REVISE EDEXCEL GCSE
German

REVISION WORKBOOK

Series Consultant: Harry Smith

Authors: Olwyn Bowpitt, Alan O'Brien, Oliver Gray

A note from the publisher

Contents

1-to-1 page match with the German Revision Guide ISBN 9781446903421

Audio files

Audio files for the listening exercises in this book can be found at: www.pearsonschools.co.uk/mflrevisionaudio

A small bit of small print

Edexcel publishes Sample Assessment Material and the Specification on its website. This is the official content and this book should be used in conjunction with it. The questions in this book have been written to help you practise what you have learned in your revision. Remember: the real exam questions may not look like this.

Target grades

Target grades are quoted in this book for some of the questions. Students targeting this grade should be aiming to get some of the marks available. Students targeting a higher grade should be aiming to get all of the marks available.

Birthdays

 Birthdays

G

1   Mia has made a note of friends' birthdays.

Julia	16. März
Marie	1. Juli
Felix	24. Januar
Leni	11. Dezember
David	12. Mai
Frank	20. Februar

> Start with the items you can do most easily.

Which month are their birthdays in? Put a cross in the correct box.

		Julia	Marie	Felix	Leni	David	Frank
Example:	January			X			
(a)	May						
(b)	July						
(c)	March						
(d)	February						

(Total for Question 1 = 4 marks)

 Birthday parties

> **Audio files**
> Audio files can be found at:
> www.pearsonschools.co.uk/mflrevisionaudio

C

2   Mrs Schulz is talking about how her family celebrate birthdays in different ways. Who does each statement refer to?
Listen and put a cross in **four** boxes.

	Mrs Schulz	Mr Schulz	Markus	Sabine
Example: Likes birthday parties	X			
(a) Doesn't celebrate birthdays				
(b) Bought some flowers				
(c) Had a sleepover				
(d) Finds birthday celebrations important				

(Total for Question 2 = 4 marks)

Physical description

Describing someone

E   3   Read the description of this person.

> # WIR SUCHEN MICHAEL HENNING
>
> **Er ist 1,70 m groß und sehr schlank. Er hat braune, glatte Haare und ein rundes Gesicht.**
>
> **Seine Augen sind grün und er trägt immer eine Brille. Er hat einen langen Bart.**
>
> **Er hat auch einen großen Ohrring im linken Ohr.**

What does he look like? Look at these possible options.

A grey	**D** long	**G** short
B curly	**E** 1.70 metres	**H** straight
C necklace	**F** green	**I** earring

Complete the grid. Enter the correct letter.

Example: Height	E
(i) Hair style	
(ii) Colour of eyes	
(iii) Style of beard	
(iv) Jewellery	

(Total for Question 3 = 4 marks)

A new girlfriend

E   4   Christian is talking about his new girlfriend. Listen and note details for the following.

Example: Name	Anna
(a) Hair	
(b) Height	
(c) Age	
(d) Wears earrings, but no…	

(Total for Question 4 = 4 marks)

Character description

Emine's brother

C

5   Emine describes her brother.

> Mein jüngerer Bruder Kadir ist dreizehn Jahre alt und wir verstehen uns wirklich gut. Als er sehr klein war, war er schüchtern und ziemlich ernst. Ich fand ihn so lieb!
>
> Kadir ist jetzt ganz lustig und freundlich. Ich finde ihn nicht mehr schüchtern. Ich bin ein bisschen faul, aber Kadir ist intelligent und in der Schule ist er immer sehr fleißig. Er ist drei Jahre jünger als ich, aber er hilft mir manchmal mit der Schularbeit.
>
> Er ist normalerweise sehr gut gelaunt, aber ab und zu wird er böse, wenn jemand unfreundlich oder ungeduldig ist.

What is Kadir like? Put a cross next to the **four** correct statements.

Kadir…

Example:	is younger than Emine.	X
(a)	and Emine get on well.	
(b)	is shy.	
(c)	used to be quite serious.	
(d)	is funny.	
(e)	is a bit lazy.	
(f)	always helps Emine with homework.	
(g)	often gets cross.	
(h)	doesn't like impatient people.	

> Make sure that you read the whole text. Don't just look for key vocabulary.

(Total for Question 5 = 4 marks)

My family

E

6   Renate is talking about her family. What does she say? Listen and put a cross in the correct box.

Example: Renate is …

   A   funny   ☒   B   impatient   ☐   C   helpful   ☐

(i) She is also…

   A   unfriendly   ☐   B   impatient   ☐   C   sporty   ☐

(ii) Jens is…

   A   hard-working   ☐   B   very friendly   ☐   C   often moody   ☐

(iii) Yesterday Jens was…

   A   tired   ☐   B   angry   ☐   C   happy   ☐

(iv) Renate's father was…

   A   angry   ☐   B   helpful   ☐   C   patient   ☐

(Total for Question 6 = 4 marks)

ID

Profiles

D 7 You read these profiles in a magazine.

> *Jusuf:* Ich habe in einer modernen Wohnung gewohnt, aber jetzt wohne ich in einem alten Haus in Hamburg.
>
> *Elias:* Ich heiße Elias, aber meine Freunde sagen Eli. Meine Mutter ist Engländerin.
>
> *Maria:* Ich wohne mit meiner Mutter in einer schönen Wohnung in Bremen.
>
> *Susi:* Ich heiße Susi und bin sechzehn Jahre alt. Mein Vater kommt aus England.
>
> *Leila:* Ich wohne in Berlin, aber ich habe sechs Jahre in Griechenland gewohnt.
>
> *Adam:* Ich bin am vierten Oktober 1999 in Hamburg geboren.

Put a cross in the **four** correct boxes.

	Jusuf	Elias	Maria	Susi	Leila	Adam
Example: Who was born in Hamburg?						X
(a) Who has a nickname?						
(b) Who has an English father?						
(c) Who has lived abroad?						
(d) Who lives in a flat?						

(Total for Question 7 = 4 marks)

Personal details

D 8 What do Hannes and Freddy say about their personal details? Listen and put a cross in the **four** correct boxes for either Hannes or Freddy.

	Hannes	Freddy
Example: I was born in Bonn.	X	
(a) My birthday is at the start of the month.		
(b) I am Swiss.		
(c) My dad is English.		
(d) I live in a flat.		
(e) I am Austrian.		

(Total for Question 8 = 4 marks)

> Be careful – there is one extra sentence, so you won't put a cross by every sentence.

Countries

Where I live

D 9 Read part of Ali's email to his new penfriend.

> Löschen Antworten Antworten Alle Weiher Drueken
>
> Ich bin sechzehn Jahre alt. Meine Eltern kommen aus der Türkei, aber ich bin in Deutschland geboren. Ich bin also Deutscher und spreche Deutsch und Türkisch.
>
> Seit 2009 wohnen wir in einer kleinen Wohnung in Berlin-Kreuzberg. Ich wohne gern hier, weil ich viele Freunde habe.
>
> 2010 habe ich meine Großeltern in der Türkei besucht. Ihr Haus ist schön, aber ich finde unsere Wohnung besser.

Put a cross by the **four** correct statements.

Example:	Ali is 16.	X
A	His parents are Turkish.	
B	Ali is Turkish.	
C	He was born in Germany.	
D	He speaks two languages.	
E	He doesn't like Berlin.	
F	He doesn't have many friends.	
G	His grandparents live in Turkey.	
H	His grandparents live in a flat.	

> Read the statements very carefully and look for details in the text.

(Total for Question 9 = 4 marks)

A new home

A 10 Silke is describing her new home. Listen and answer the questions in **English**.

   (a) What did Silke particularly like about Munich? Give **two** details.

   (i) ....

   .... (1 mark)

   (ii) ....

   .... (1 mark)

   (b) What does she think about where she lives now?

   (i) Positive: ....

   .... (1 mark)

   (ii) Negative: ....

   .... (1 mark)

(Total for Question 10 = 4 marks)

Brothers and sisters

Brothers and sisters

11 You read this profile in a magazine, about Sophie's family members.

> Sophies Bruder ist sieben Jahre alt und ihre Schwester ist dreizehn. Sie muss ziemlich oft auf ihren Bruder aufpassen und sie findet ihn sehr lustig. Er ist manchmal ein bisschen frech, aber sie verstehen sich gut.
>
> Sie findet ihre Schwester aber ganz nervig. Sie nimmt manchmal Sophies Sachen, zum Beispiel Kleidung und CDs. Und sie spielt laute Musik, wenn Sophie lesen oder lernen will. Sie streiten sich die ganze Zeit.

A	kind	D	playing	G	funny
B	annoying	E	a sister	H	well
C	badly	F	arguing	I	cheeky

Fill in the missing information. Write the correct letter.

Example: Sophie has a brother and ...E... .

(i) Her brother is sometimes ....

(ii) She and her brother generally get on ....

(iii) She finds her sister ....

(iv) She and her sister are always ....

(Total for Question 11 = 4 marks)

  My sister

12 Alex has a problem with his sister. Complete the sentences by entering the correct letter at the end of each sentence.

A	different	D	one TV	G	paid for it
B	his toys	E	similar	H	her dolls
C	is a teenager	F	sister	I	a broken TV

Write the **four** correct letters in the spaces below.

Example: Alex doesn't get on well with his ...F... .

(i) Alex is complaining because he and his sister are so ....

(ii) It annoys him that his sister always plays with ....

(iii) The problem is that there is only ....

(iv) Alex thinks he should be allowed to watch TV because he ....

(Total for Question 12 = 4 marks)

> Before you listen, think about which words would fit in each gap. You will be able to focus your listening more if you are well prepared.

Family

 Family life

13 You read this article in a newspaper.

> Ich bin ein Einzelkind, aber ich fühle mich gar nicht einsam. Als ich klein war, haben wir in Frankfurt gewohnt. In derselben Stadt haben meine Großeltern und meine Tanten gewohnt, und es hat mir viel Spaß gemacht, regelmäßig mit meinen zwei Cousinen zu spielen.
>
> Weil meine Eltern bis spät am Abend arbeiten mussten, hat meine Tante Julia nach der Schule auf mich aufgepasst. Meine Tante ist ebenso streng wie meine Mutter und mein Vater, und ich musste immer Hausaufgaben machen, bevor ich spielen oder fernsehen durfte. Das war mir egal, weil mir meine Cousine oft geholfen hat, die Schularbeiten fertig zu schreiben.
>
> Vor vier Jahren mussten wir nach Bonn umziehen und jetzt wohnen wir weit von der Familie entfernt. Wir sehen uns zwar nicht so oft, aber wir können telefonieren oder mailen. Außerdem organisiert meine Mutter in den Sommerferien oft einen Familienausflug. Jedes Jahr unternehmen wir etwas Neues und die ganze Familie macht mit.
>
> **Thomas (16)**

(a) Choose the correct ending for each statement.

(i) Thomas hat…	**A** verbrachte er viel Zeit mit der Familie.
(ii) Als kleines Kind…	**B** keine Geschwister.
(iii) Abends…	**C** ist die Familie umgezogen.
(iv) Als er Schularbeiten machte, …	**D** waren seine Eltern beschäftigt.
(v) Als er zwölf war, …	**E** hat er einen Ausflug gemacht.
	F war seine Cousine hilfsbereit.

Example: (i) …B…

(ii) ....   **(iii)** ....   **(iv)** ....   **(v)** ....

(b) Put a cross by the **four** correct statements.

Example:	Thomas fühlt sich nicht allein.	X
(i)	Er hat gern mit seinen Cousinen gespielt.	
(ii)	Er hat als kleines Kind in Bonn gewohnt.	
(iii)	Seine Tante war nicht sehr streng.	
(iv)	Er war jeden Abend bei seiner Tante.	
(v)	Er wohnt jetzt in einer anderen Stadt.	
(vi)	Er spricht nicht mit seiner Familie.	
(vii)	Er ruft seine Cousinen jedes Jahr an.	
(viii)	Die ganze Familie trifft sich jedes Jahr.	

(Total for Question 13 = 8 marks)

Friends

 My friends

C   **14** Read what these young people think about their friends.

> **Ahmed** ist treu und humorvoll. Er hilft gerne, wenn jemand ein Problem hat.
>
> **Max** ist ein guter Freund, aber er ist manchmal launisch. Er wird böse, wenn er ein
>
> Spiel nicht gewinnt.
>
> **Lena** ist sehr lustig, aber ziemlich laut. Sie ist nie schlecht gelaunt und ist so nett.
>
> **Ralf** ist sehr intelligent und schüchtern. Wir verstehen uns gut.
>
> **Hanna** ist sehr fleißig. Sie arbeitet viel in der Schule und zu Hause.
>
> **Frank** liebt Musik. Er spielt Gitarre und singt die ganze Zeit.

Who is it? Write the correct name in the box.

Example: Who is shy?	Ralf
(a) Who likes to win games?	
(b) Who is happy to help others?	
(c) Who is hard-working?	
(d) Who is never in a bad mood?	

> Look out for **relevant** detail, not just the most obvious answer.

(Total for Question 14 = 4 marks)

 School friends

B   **15** Melissa has been visiting some of her old school friends.

How have her friends changed? Listen and enter the correct letter.

A | Funny   **C** | Quiet   **E** | Shy

B | Annoying   **D** | Friendly   **F** | Cheeky

	Previously	Now
Ivan	Example: C	**(ii)**
	(i)	
Olivia	**(iii)**	**(iv)**

(Total for Question 15 = 4 marks)

Hobbies

Whose hobby?

F

16 Read what these young people like doing in their spare time.

Susi	Ich spiele gern Gitarre.
Fabian	Mein Hobby ist Schlittschuhlaufen.
Adam	Am Wochenende angle ich im See.
Lara	Ich finde Leichtathletik toll.
Ali	Ich wandere gern in den Bergen.
Teresa	Jeden Freitag gehe ich schwimmen.

> Make sure that you look for the key vocabulary within each sentence.

Whose hobby is this? Put a cross in the correct box.

		Susi	Fabian	Adam	Lara	Ali	Teresa
Example:	Guitar	X					
(a)	Hiking						
(b)	Ice skating						
(c)	Swimming						
(d)	Fishing						

(Total for Question 16 = 4 marks)

Young people and hobbies

F

17 What hobbies do these young people have?

Listen and put a cross in the correct box.

	A	B	C	D	E	F
Example: Mohammed				X		
(i) Fiona						
(ii) Max						
(iii) Brigitte						
(iv) Stefan						

(Total for Question 17 = 4 marks)

Sports

 **Sport**

G 18 Look at these different sports.

Fußball   Schwimmen   Reiten   Tischtennis   Skifahren

Put a cross next to the **four** other sports listed above.

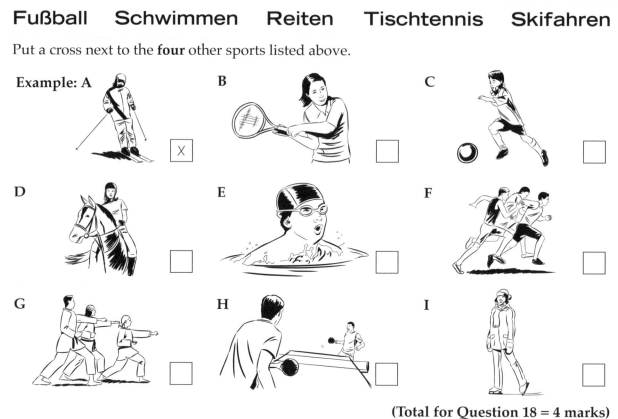

Example: A [X]

B ☐

C ☐

D ☐

E ☐

F ☐

G ☐

H ☐

I ☐

(Total for Question 18 = 4 marks)

 Opinions about sport

D 19 How do Gabi and Julia view sport? Listen and put a cross in the **four** correct boxes for either Gabi or Julia.

	Gabi	Julia
Example: I am a sports fan	X	
(a) Sport is tiring.		
(b) I prefer sport video games.		
(c) I play for a team.		
(d) I love basketball.		
(e) I never do sport.		

(Total for Question 19 = 4 marks)

Arranging to go out

An invitation

20 Salma has invited her friends to go to the cinema. Read their replies.

> Ich kann nicht ins Kino gehen, weil ich Fieber und Kopfschmerzen habe. Ich muss eine Woche zu Hause bleiben. **Maria**

> Toll! Ich komme mit! Aber ich muss vorher meine Oma besuchen. Ich treffe dich um halb acht im Kino. **Ralf**

> Ich habe den Film letzte Woche schon gesehen. Er war gut, aber ich will ihn nicht zweimal sehen! **Fatima**

> Ich möchte lieber einen Liebesfilm sehen. Tut mir leid. **Sara**

> Ich spiele am Samstag in Frankfurt Hockey. Leider kommen wir erst abends um 10 Uhr nach Hause. **Adam**

Who says what? Put a cross in the correct box.

		Maria	Ralf	Fatima	Sara	Adam
Example:	I've already seen it.			X		
(a)	I'd rather see a romantic film.					
(b)	I'm too ill.					
(c)	I'm playing sport.					
(d)	I'll see you at 7.30.					

(Total for Question 20 = 4 marks)

Where are they going?

21 What are their plans? Listen and put a cross in the correct box.

Example: They are going…

A to school ☐

B to the pool ☐

C to the cinema ☒

(i) They are going…

  A to the park ☐

  B to visit friends ☐

  C to the youth club ☐

(ii) They are going…

  A dancing ☐

  B swimming ☐

  C bowling ☐

(iii) They are going…

  A cycling ☐

  B swimming ☐

  C to a café ☐

(iv) They are going…

  A rollerskating ☐

  B swimming ☐

  C cycling ☐

(Total for Question 21 = 4 marks)

Last weekend

Jusuf's weekend

B 22 Read part of Jusuf's blog about last weekend.

> Normalerweise mache ich am Wochenende nicht viel, weil ich viele Schularbeiten habe. Aber letztes Wochenende war fantastisch.
>
> Weil mein Freund Peter Geburtstag hatte, sind wir am Samstag in ein neues Zentrum gegangen, wo man viele tolle Aktivitäten machen kann.
>
> Wir sind mit dem Auto dorthin gefahren und Peters Vater hat die Eintrittskarten gekauft. Am Vormittag bin ich reiten gegangen. Ich fand Reiten toll, obwohl ich nicht so gut war. Es war nicht leicht!
>
> Am Nachmittag ist Peter geklettert, und ich bin Skateboard gefahren. Ich bin mehrmals hingefallen und jetzt tun meine Knie weh! Danach sind wir beide in einem kleinen Boot auf dem See gesegelt. Es war ein toller Tag.

What does he say about last weekend? Put a cross in the correct box.

Example: At the weekend Jusuf usually…

(i)	does his homework.	X
(ii)	goes out.	
(iii)	visits Peter.	

(a) Last weekend was…

(i)	the same as usual.	
(ii)	different.	
(iii)	Jusuf's birthday.	

(c) Jusuf found horse-riding…

(i)	easy.	
(ii)	great.	
(iii)	not very good.	

(b) The outing was paid for by…

(i)	Jusuf.	
(ii)	Peter.	
(iii)	Peter's father.	

(d) Jusuf hurt himself…

(i)	sailing.	
(ii)	climbing.	
(iii)	skateboarding.	

(Total for Question 22 = 4 marks)

Leisure time

B 23 Thomas describes his leisure interests. What did he do last weekend and what are his plans for next weekend? Enter the correct letter in the table below.

A	Walking	C	Going to the cinema	E	Playing computer games
B	Shopping	D	Restaurant	F	Swimming

Last weekend	Next weekend
Example: B	
(i)	(iii)
(ii)	(iv)

(Total for Question 23 = 4 marks)

TV programmes

TV programmes

F

24 Read these comments about TV programmes.

„Viele Seifenopern sind langweilig."

„Am Freitag gibt es einen tollen Krimi. "

„Jeden Nachmittag gibt es einen Zeichentrickfilm. "

„Die besten Sendungen sind Komödien. "

„Meine Eltern finden die Nachrichten interessant. "

Which sorts of programme are mentioned? Put a cross in the **four** correct boxes.

Example:	Soaps	X
(a)	News	
(b)	Cartoons	
(c)	Horror films	
(d)	Documentaries	
(e)	Comedies	
(f)	Romantic films	
(g)	Detective stories	
(h)	Quiz shows	

(Total for Question 24 = 4 marks)

Favourite programmes

C

25 What do these people enjoy watching on television? Listen and put a cross in four boxes.

	Jonas	Lena	Felix	Sofia	Luca
Example: Sports shows	X				
(a) Current affairs					
(b) Nothing					
(c) Funny programmes					
(d) Thrillers					

(Total for Question 25 = 4 marks)

Look at options (a)–(d) before you listen and try to predict what vocabulary you are going to hear.

Cinema

A German film

A 26 You read this film review in a magazine.

> Keep your answers short and relevant.

★★★

Der deutsche Abenteuerfilm *Yoko* ist im Februar 2012 in die Kinos gekommen. Im Film geht es um die Freundschaft zwischen einem Yeti, Yoko, und einem deutschen Mädchen, Pia. Yoko wohnt in den Bergen des Himalajas, aber eines Tages kommt er in Deutschland an, wo Pia ihn findet. Die beiden werden feste Freunde. Leider ist Deutschland zu warm für Yoko und Pia muss ihm helfen, in seine Heimat* zurückzukehren.

Yoko ist ein Film für die ganze Familie. Die Geschichte ist lustig und spannend. Es gibt schöne Effekte, Computeranimationen und tolle Musik. Jamie Bick spielt die Rolle von Pia. *Yoko* ist ihr erster Film. Einige Kritiker finden, dass sie viel besser als die Erwachsenen im Film ist. Weil der Film auf Deutsch ist, braucht man keine Untertitel und keine Synchronisation.

* homeland

Answer the following questions in **English.** You do not need to write in sentences.

(a) What sort of film is it? .... **(1 mark)**

(b) Where does Yoko normally live? .... **(1 mark)**

(c) How do Pia and Yoko get on? .... **(1 mark)**

(d) Why does Yoko go back home? .... **(1 mark)**

(e) Who is the film suitable for? .... **(1 mark)**

(f) How many films has Jamie Bick been in? .... **(1 mark)**

(g) What do some critics say about her? .... **(1 mark)**

(h) Why are subtitles unnecessary? .... **(1 mark)**

(Total for Question 26 = 8 marks)

A trip to the cinema

A 27 Alfred is describing a trip to the cinema. Listen and answer the questions in **English.**

(a) Where exactly was the cinema?

.... **(1 mark)**

(b) How did Alfred hear about the film?

.... **(1 mark)**

(c) What did he particularly like about the film?

.... **(1 mark)**

(d) Why did he go on Wednesday?

.... **(1 mark)**

(Total for Question 27 = 4 marks)

Music

 A German band

E

28 You read this article about Juli, a German band.

Juli ist eine Pop-Rock-Band aus Deutschland. Ihre erste Single „Perfekte Welle" war 2004 auf Platz Nummer 2 der deutschen Musikcharts. 2006 war ihr Album „Ein neuer Tag" auf Nummer 1.

Eva Briegel (Sängerin) schreibt zusammen mit Simon Triebel und Jonas Pfetzing (Gitarre) die Lieder auf Deutsch. Man hört ihre Musik sehr oft im deutschen Radio.

Answer the questions in **English**.

Example: What is the name of the band? .....Juli.................................

(a) Where does the band come from? .... (1 mark)

(b) When was their first single? .... (1 mark)

(c) Which language does Eva write the songs in? .... (1 mark)

(d) Where can you hear the band's music? .... (1 mark)

(Total for Question 28 = 4 marks)

> Keep your answers short and simple. One word is usually enough.

 Enjoying music

D

29 What musical activities did Jessica and Anja do yesterday? Listen and put a cross in the correct box for either Jessica or Anja.

	Jessica	Anja
Example: Listened to the radio	X	
(a) Played the flute		
(b) Went to a concert		
(c) Downloaded music		
(d) Sang		

(Total for Question 29 = 4 marks)

15

Had a go ☐   Nearly there ☐   Nailed it! ☐

Online activities

 Internet

A

30 You see this article about the internet.

> **Markus (16)** sucht meistens Informationen für die Schularbeiten im Internet. Oft werden seine Eltern böse, weil sie denken, dass er zu viel Zeit online verbringt.
>
> **Meryem (17)** benutzt das Internet, um stundenlang mit Freundinnen zu chatten. Das nervt ihren Bruder. Manchmal geht sie in ein Internetcafé, aber das kostet viel Geld. Zu Hause zahlen die Eltern!
>
> **Hannah (19)** sucht online Informationen über Filme. Sie findet es praktisch, weil man schnell sehen kann, welche Filme laufen und ob man sie empfehlen würde. Ab und zu kaufen sie und ihre Mutter auch Kleidung im Internet.
>
> **Thomas (15)** benutzt das Internet, um seinen Freunden in England E-Mails zu schicken. Außerdem liest er online Nachrichten oder Sportreportagen.

Answer the following questions in **English**.

(a) What does Markus use the internet for? .... **(1 mark)**

(b) How do his parents react? .... **(1 mark)**

(c) What does Meryem do online? .... **(1 mark)**

(d) What is the disadvantage of internet cafés?

.... **(1 mark)**

(e) Why does Hannah look for films online? Give **one** example.

.... **(1 mark)**

(f) What else does Hannah do online? .... **(1 mark)**

(g) What does Thomas do online? Give **two** examples.

    (i) .... **(1 mark)**

    (ii) .... **(1 mark)**

(Total for Question 30 = 8 marks)

 Young people and the internet

F

31 Listen to these people talking about what they use the internet for.

A	Playing games	**C**	Doing homework	**E**	Watching TV programmes
B	Talking to friends	**D**	Downloading music	**F**	Shopping

Choose the correct letter for each statement.

Example: ..D..........

(i) ....   **(ii)** ....   **(iii)** ....   **(iv)** ....

(Total for Question 31 = 4 marks)

Daily routine

A change to school routine

32 You hear a report on local radio about a change at a school. Listen and put a cross in the correct box.

Example: The survey was about school…

(i)	routine.	X
(ii)	uniform.	
(iii)	lunches.	

(a) Three quarters of pupils…

(i)	were happy with the school routine.	
(ii)	found the school day tiring.	
(iii)	didn't respond to the survey.	

(b) Most pupils would prefer to…

(i)	go to school on Saturdays.	
(ii)	finish school earlier.	
(iii)	start school later.	

(c) Teachers are keen…

(i)	to improve students' grades.	
(ii)	to cut the short break.	
(iii)	to have shorter assemblies.	

(d) This teacher thinks changing the school routine…

(i)	will definitely improve pupils' behaviour.	
(ii)	is not a good idea.	
(iii)	will probably have no effect on pupils' behaviour.	

(Total for Question 32 = 4 marks)

Breakfast

 Breakfast

Ⓓ **33** Read these statements.

> *Leila*: Während der Woche frühstücke ich nicht, weil ich zu spät aufstehe. Am Wochenende trinke ich gern Kakao und ich esse Müsli.

> *Ahmed*: Zum Frühstück essen wir Brot mit Käse. Ich trinke Fruchtsaft und meine Eltern trinken Kaffee.

> *Felix*: Ich esse immer Brot mit Marmelade und ich trinke Milch. Ich trinke keinen Kaffee oder Tee.

What does each person have for breakfast? Put a cross in the correct box.

		Leila	Ahmed	Felix
Example:	Fruit juice		X	
(a)	Nothing on weekdays			
(b)	Milk			
(c)	Cheese			
(d)	Bread and jam			

(Total for Question 33 = 4 marks)

🎧17 **Breakfast at the hotel**

Ⓓ **34** Mr Schreiber is asking about breakfast at the hotel.

A fruit juice	**D** € 13	**G** eggs
B meat	**E** what's for breakfast	**H** coffee
C tea	**F** hot chocolate	**I** € 10

Write the **four** correct letters in the boxes below.

Example: Mr Schreiber wants to know ⬚E⬚ .

(i) To drink there is ⬚ and ⬚ .

(ii) To eat there is ⬚ .

(iii) Breakfast costs ⬚ per person.

> Look first at which words or phrases will fit sensibly into each gap. That will reduce your options for each one.

(Total for Question 34 = 4 marks)

Eating at home

Mealtimes

C

35 Read this article about eating at home.

> Tom (15):
>
> Das Frühstück zu Hause ist oft sehr stressig, weil wir nicht viel Zeit haben. Wir essen oder trinken ganz schnell etwas und verlassen um halb acht das Haus.
>
> Das Abendessen ist viel ruhiger. Wir essen in der Woche um achtzehn Uhr und am Wochenende um neunzehn Uhr.
>
> Es gibt ziemlich oft Nudeln, weil die ganze Familie sie mag. Man kann Nudeln ganz schnell zubereiten. Wir essen nicht gern Reis. Mein Lieblingsessen ist Schweinefleisch mit Kohl. Das ist lecker. Mein Bruder liebt Bratwurst mit Bohnen oder Karotten, aber er mag keinen Kohl. Ich esse nicht gern Omelett oder Salat.

Put a cross in the correct box.

(a) The evening meal is…

(i)	calmer.	
(ii)	more stressful.	
(iii)	busier.	

(b) At the weekend the evening meal is at…

(i)	6.00 pm.	
(ii)	7.30 pm.	
(iii)	7.00 pm.	

(c) Everyone in Tom's family likes…

(i)	pasta.	
(ii)	cabbage.	
(iii)	rice.	

(d) Tom's favourite meal is…

(i)	sausage with beans.	
(ii)	pork with cabbage.	
(iii)	omelette with salad.	

(Total for Question 35 = 4 marks)

A family visit

C

36 Laura is describing a visit to her cousin. Listen and put a cross in the correct box.

Example: When was Laura's visit?

(i) last week ☒   **(ii)** last year ☐   **(iii)** two years ago ☐

(a) What did she usually eat for breakfast?

(i)	cheese and bread	
(ii)	bread and ham	
(iii)	strawberries	

(b) What did she particularly enjoy?

(i)	chocolate cake	
(ii)	coffee	
(iii)	cream	

(c) What is her favourite food?

(i)	pasta and cheese	
(ii)	sandwiches	
(iii)	pasta and salad	

(d) What will she make for her cousin?

(i)	chicken salad	
(ii)	fish and chips	
(iii)	a roast	

(Total for Question 36 = 4 marks)

Had a go ☐ Nearly there ☐ Nailed it! ☐

Healthy eating

A healthy lifestyle

B

37 You read this article on the internet.

Wie bleibst du fit?

Ben: Um fit zu bleiben, spiele ich dreimal in der Woche Hockey und ich gehe jeden Samstag schwimmen.

Adam: Ich koche leckere und gesunde Mahlzeiten ohne zu viel Salz oder Fett.

Mina: Als ich jünger war, war ich sehr faul und nicht sehr gesund. Jetzt esse ich gesund und ich trainiere zweimal in der Woche. Ich habe viel mehr Energie.

Sara: Ich trinke viel Wasser und ich esse gesund. Ich rauche nicht, weil es gefährlich ist.

Leila: Ich gehe zu Fuß zur Schule und ich fahre oft Rad. Ich spare Geld und bleibe fit!

Tom: Meiner Meinung nach ist es sehr leicht, fit zu bleiben, wenn man mit Freunden trainiert.

Who says the following? Write the correct name in the table below.

Example:	I drink plenty of water.	Sara
(a)	I cook healthy food.	
(b)	I think it is easier to keep fit with friends.	
(c)	I do a lot of sport.	
(d)	I eat more healthily than I used to.	

(Total for Question 37 = 4 marks)

Health and fitness

A*

38 You hear a report on the radio. What does Dr Huth say? Listen and put a cross in the **four** correct boxes.

Example: Dr Huth is discussing diet.	X
(a) You shouldn't eat chicken.	
(b) You can eat red meat occasionally.	
(c) A vegetarian diet is not to be recommended.	
(d) The best diet includes fish.	
(e) You shouldn't eat bread for breakfast.	
(f) White bread is best avoided.	
(g) Our grandparents drank too much milk.	
(h) Milk should be drunk in small quantities.	

(Total for Question 38 = 4 marks)

Keeping fit

Fitness camps

A*

39 You read this magazine article about fitness camps.

> ## Bist du 11–16 Jahre alt? Machst du dir Sorgen um deine Gesundheit?
>
> Vielleicht solltest du in unser Jugend-Fitness-Camp kommen! Hier kannst du coole Leute aus Deutschland und ganz Europa kennen lernen und neue Freundschaften schließen.
>
> Dieses Camp ist ein Muss für alle, die vom Computer weg wollen. Bei uns gibt es verschiedene Aktivitäten in der Turnhalle und auf dem Sportplatz. Abends kannst du chillen. Am Wochenende machst du spannende Ausflüge in die nähere Umgebung.
>
> Unser Angebot:
> * bequeme Schlafzimmer für bis zu vier Jugendliche
> * Vollpension mit frischen, vitaminreichen Speisen
> * tägliche Morgengymnastik, die dich in Bewegung bringt
> * Spaziergänge und Radtouren an der frischen Luft. Nach einem Mittagsschlaf gibt es Gruppendiskussionen darüber, wie man auch zu Hause weiter gesund leben kann.

What is said about the fitness camps? Put a cross in the correct box.

(a) Die Fitness-Camp-Kunden sind…

(i)	nur aus Deutschland.	
(ii)	aus der ganzen Welt.	
(iii)	aus vielen europäischen Ländern.	

(b) Man sollte das Camp besuchen, wenn man…

(i)	zu viel am Computer arbeitet.	
(ii)	Computerspiele machen will.	
(iii)	etwas über Computer lernen will.	

(c) Am Abend kann man…

(i)	sich entspannen.	
(ii)	für sich selbst kochen.	
(iii)	am Computer spielen.	

(d) Am Wochenende…

(i)	fährt man nach Hause.	
(ii)	geht man einkaufen.	
(iii)	sieht man die Gegend.	

(e) Im Schlafzimmer gibt es…

(i)	nicht mehr als vier Personen.	
(ii)	vier Personen.	
(iii)	mehr als vier Personen.	

(f) Im Angebot bekommt man…

(i)	nur Frühstück.	
(ii)	keine Mahlzeiten.	
(iii)	alle Mahlzeiten.	

(g) Nach dem Mittagessen…

(i)	geht man joggen.	
(ii)	ruht man sich aus.	
(iii)	sieht man fern.	

(h) In den Gruppendiskussionen bespricht man…

(i)	die Verhältnisse im Camp.	
(ii)	die Pläne für den nächsten Tag.	
(iii)	einen gesunden Lebensstil.	

(Total for Question 39 = 8 marks)

Illness

Illnesses

40 These people have various things wrong with them.

Susi:	Ich habe Kopfschmerzen.
Fabian:	Ich habe eine Grippe. Ich bin sehr krank.
Adam:	Ich habe heute Fieber.
Lara:	Jetzt tun meine Beine weh.
Ali:	Ich habe starke Magenschmerzen.
Teresa:	Ich bleibe zu Hause. Ich habe Husten.

> Make sure that you look for the key vocabulary within each sentence.

What is the problem? Put a cross in the correct box.

Who has …

		Susi	Fabian	Adam	Lara	Ali	Teresa
Example:	a headache?	X					
(a)	stomach-ache?						
(b)	flu?						
(c)	a cough?						
(d)	a temperature?						

(Total for Question 40 = 4 marks)

At the doctor's

41 What is wrong with these people?

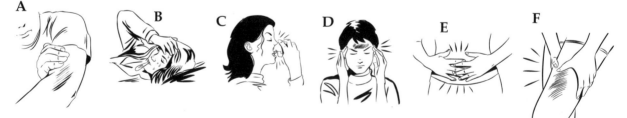

Listen and put a cross in the correct box.

	A	B	C	D	E	F
Example: Mia	X					
(i) Sofia						
(ii) Elias						
(iii) Anna						
(iv) Max						

(Total for Question 41 = 4 marks)

Health issues

 Healthy living

F **42** Read this advice about how to stay healthy.

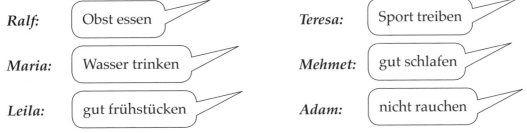

Ralf: Obst essen   *Teresa:* Sport treiben

Maria: Wasser trinken   *Mehmet:* gut schlafen

Leila: gut frühstücken   *Adam:* nicht rauchen

Who gives advice about what? Write the correct name in the box.

Example: sport?	Teresa
(i) sleep	
(ii) fruit	
(iii) smoking	
(iv) water	

(Total for Question 42 = 4 marks)

 Karl's grandparents

C **43** Karl is describing a visit to his grandparents. Put a cross in the correct box.

Example: Which day is Karl describing?

(i)	Monday.	
(ii)	Sunday.	X
(iii)	Wednesday.	

Be careful with multiple-choice questions. Words from each option may be in the text but you have to listen to the detail to get the correct answer.

(a) How many cigarettes does Karl's grandmother smoke?

(i)	Ten a day.	
(ii)	None.	
(iii)	Twenty a day.	

(b) Why does Karl prefer the park?

(i)	It's far away from the flat.	
(ii)	The air is better.	
(iii)	His grandad drives him there.	

(c) What does his grandfather have at the café?

(i)	Nothing.	
(ii)	An ice cream and a coffee.	
(iii)	A weak coffee.	

(d) How old is Karl's grandfather?

(i)	77.	
(ii)	71.	
(iii)	70.	

(Total for Question 43 = 4 marks)

At the tourist office

At the tourist office

D 1 You read this notice in the visitor centre.

Herzlich willkommen!

In unserer Stadt kann man viel machen.

Das interessante Stadtmuseum ist von Dienstag bis Sonntag 10:30–16:30 Uhr geöffnet. Der Eintritt kostet €6, aber es gibt eine Ermäßigung für Kinder und Studenten.

Nächsten Sonntag kann man einen Ausflug in die wunderbare Stadt Bonn machen. Wir fahren um 8:30 Uhr vom Busbahnhof ab.

Die tolle Kunstgalerie im Rathaus ist von 10:00 bis 17:00 Uhr geöffnet. Sie ist montags geschlossen.

Am Donnerstag gibt es eine Rundfahrt durch die Stadt. Die Rundfahrt beginnt um 11:00 Uhr am Dom und ist perfekt für Kinder.

What does the town offer? Complete the information by choosing the correct letter.

A	Thursday–Sunday	D	interesting	G	Tuesday–Sunday
B	cathedral	E	town hall	H	children
C	train station	F	students	I	bus station

Example: The museum is ...D....

(i)   The museum is open ....

(ii) The Bonn trip leaves from the ....

(iii) The art gallery is in the ....

(iv) The tour of the town is great for ....

(Total for Question 1 = 4 marks)

What to see and do

C 2 Frank is at the tourist information office. He wants to know what there is to see and do.

Complete the sentences by putting a cross (x) in the correct box.

Example: Most people go first to the...

(i)	museum.	
(ii)	cathedral.	X
(iii)	zoo.	

(a) The exhibition is open until...

(i)	Friday.	
(ii)	Saturday.	
(iii)	Sunday.	

(b) The museum has an exhibition of...

(i)	modern art.	
(ii)	children's pictures.	
(iii)	old bicycles.	

(c) Hiring a bike is...

(i)	expensive.	
(ii)	not possible.	
(iii)	cheap.	

(d) Frank could return to the information office to...

(i)	get some brochures.	
(ii)	book theatre tickets.	
(iii)	buy a town map.	

(Total for Question 2 = 4 marks)

What to do in town

Visiting Bremen

A   3   Read the following article about Bremen.

Bremen

Jedes Jahr gibt es in Bremen viele Touristen und sie kommen oft noch einmal zurück. Warum? Weil diese norddeutsche Stadt so viel bietet: Geschichte, tolle Einkaufsmöglichkeiten, ein gutes Nachtleben, schöne Spaziergänge.

Sie finden hier preiswerte Unterkunft, aber während des Weihnachtsmarktes sollten Sie im Voraus buchen, weil Hotels und auch Jugendherbergen schnell ausgebucht sind.

Mit der „Erlebniscard Bremen" kann man mit öffentlichen Verkehrsmitteln billiger fahren. Außerdem bekommt man mit dieser Karte eine Ermäßigung für das Theater, Führungen usw.

Im Schnoorviertel finden Sie allerlei interessante Geschäfte, wo Sie Andenken oder Geschenke kaufen können. Danach sollten Sie in den Cafés und Restaurants die Spezialitäten der Stadt genießen.

Jeder Besucher wird in den vielen verschiedenen Museen etwas Interessantes finden. Vergessen Sie aber nicht, dass die meisten Museen montags geschlossen sind.

Answer the questions in **English**. You do not need to answer in full sentences.

> Keep your answers short and relevant.

(a) What do visitors often do?

.... **(1 mark)**

(b) Where is Bremen?

.... **(1 mark)**

(c) What advice is given about accommodation during the Christmas market?

.... **(1 mark)**

(d) What does the *Erlebniscard Bremen* offer?

(i) .... **(1 mark)**

(ii) .... **(1 mark)**

(e) Give **two** different things to do in the *Schnoorviertel*.

(i) .... **(1 mark)**

(ii) .... **(1 mark)**

(f) When couldn't you visit most museums?

.... **(1 mark)**

(Total for Question 3 = 8 marks)

Signs around town

Signs in town

F   4   You see these signs in town.

A
Der Schnellimbiss ist jeden Tag geöffnet.

C
Das Restaurant ist heute geschlossen.

E
Sie dürfen hier nicht parken.

B
Kinder sind im Museum immer willkommen.

D
Die Toiletten sind neben dem Eingang.

F
Im Bahnhof darf man nicht rauchen.

Which sign is it? Write the correct letter in the box.

Example:	Toilets	D
(i)	Children welcome	
(ii)	No smoking	
(iii)	Closed today	
(iv)	No parking	

(Total for Question 4 = 4 marks)

Visiting Berlin

E   5   You read this advertisement for a travel card.

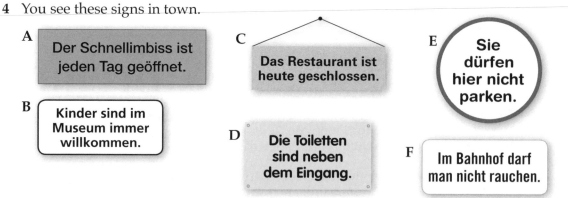

Berlin WelcomeCard

Das Touristen-Ticket

▶ Mit der Berlin WelcomeCard können Touristen 72 Stunden lang mit allen öffentlichen Verkehrsmitteln in der ganzen Stadt fahren.

▶ Kinder unter 6 Jahren fahren kostenlos mit.

▶ Man kann die WelcomeCard am Bahnhof oder am Flughafen kaufen.

Answer these questions in **English**.

(a) Who is this ticket aimed at? .... **(1 mark)**

(b) Where can you use it? .... **(1 mark)**

(c) Who travels free? .... **(1 mark)**

(d) Where can you buy this ticket? Give **one** example. .... **(1 mark)**

(Total for Question 5 = 4 marks)

At the station

At the train station

G 6 Which sign is it? Put the correct letter in the box.

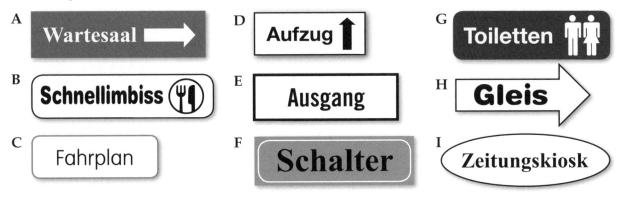

A Wartesaal ➡

B Schnellimbiss 🍴

C Fahrplan

D Aufzug ⬆

E Ausgang

F Schalter

G Toiletten

H Gleis

I Zeitungskiosk

Example:	Toilet	G
(i)	Tickets	
(ii)	Timetable	
(iii)	The waiting room	
(iv)	The exit	

(Total for Question 6 = 4 marks)

Places at the station

F 7 These people are asking for directions at the station. Where do they want to go?

A underground

B exit

C taxi

D waiting room

E platform

F ticket office

Put a cross under the correct letter.

	A	**B**	**C**	**D**	**E**	**F**
Example:			X			
(i)						
(ii)						
(iii)						
(iv)						

(Total for Question 7 = 4 marks)

Weather

 Weather

F   8   What is the weather like today in Austria?

> **A**   Am Vormittag gibt es Gewitter.
>
> **B**   Es regnet in Wien.
>
> **C**   Im Süden scheint den ganzen Tag die Sonne.
>
> **D**   Am Nachmittag ist es ziemlich kalt.
>
> **E**   Im Osten ist es warm.
>
> **F**   In der Nacht gibt es im Westen Nebel.

Look for key words in each sentence.

Write the correct letter in each box.

Example:	Rain	B
(i)	Cold	
(ii)	Thunderstorm	
(iii)	Fog	
(iv)	Sun	

(Total for Question 8 = 4 marks)

 Today's weather

E   9   Listen to this weather report.

A	sunny		**D**	cloudy

B	cold		**E**	rainy

C	windy		**F**	snowy

Write the correct letter in each box.

Example:	Hamburg	F
(i)	Dortmund	
(ii)	Bremen	
(iii)	Stuttgart	
(iv)	Berlin	

Think of the German expressions for A–F before you listen, so that you will be better prepared.

(Total for Question 9 = 4 marks)

Places in town

 Places in town

G **10** What is there in the town?

der Park	das Schloss	die Kirche	der Markt	das Kino

Put a cross in the **four** correct boxes.

> Only cross **four** boxes. You will lose marks if you cross more than four.

Example: A

☒

B

☐

C

☐

D

☐

E

☐

F

☐

G

☐

H

☐

I

☐

(Total for Question 10 = 4 marks)

  Closing time

G **11** Listen to the information. At what time do these places close?

A	post office	**C**	market	**E**	museum
B	sports centre	**D**	car park	**F**	ice rink

Put the correct letter next to the time.

Example:	10 o'clock	B
(i)	5 o'clock	
(ii)	9 o'clock	
(iii)	11 o'clock	
(iv)	6 o'clock	

(Total for Question 10 = 4 marks)

Around town

 In Berlin

F

12 What is on offer in Berlin?

Put a cross in the **four** correct boxes.

Example:	Tennis	X
(a)	Theatre	
(b)	Cinema	
(c)	Shopping	
(d)	Football	
(e)	Cathedral	
(f)	Swimming	
(g)	Zoo	
(h)	Dancing	

Kommen Sie nach

Berlin!

- Für Sportler: Im Sommer: Tennis spielen
- Für Filmfans: Modernes Kino mit den neusten Kinohits
- Für Kulturinteressierte: Historischer Dom in der Stadtmitte
- Für Familien: Freizeitzentrum mit Schwimmbad
- Für Teenager: Tanzen in Klubs

(Total for Question 12 = 4 marks)

 In town

E

13 Julia is going to show her visitor Maria around her town. Where are they going?

A	town centre
B	a café
C	the harbour

D	market
E	the cathedral
F	town hall

Write the letter of the correct place.

Example:	B
(i)	
(ii)	
(iii)	
(iv)	

(Total for Question 13 = 4 marks)

Opinions of your town

Opinions about a town

C

14 Read what these people say about their town.

> *Felix:* In meiner Stadt gibt es viele Unterhaltungsmöglichkeiten für Jugendliche: ein
> neues Freizeitzentrum, zwei Kinos, ein Theater usw. Leider gibt es viel Verkehr
> und es ist sehr laut.
>
> *Lilli:* Ich wohne in einer kleinen Stadt. Es gibt nichts zu tun, weil wir kein Kino und
> kein Sportzentrum haben. Wir fahren oft in die nächste Stadt, weil dort die
> Geschäfte gut sind.
>
> *Sophie:* Ich liebe meine Stadt, aber im Sommer gibt es zu viele Touristen. Dann sind die
> Staus so lang und die Cafés am Marktplatz sind immer voll.

Put a cross in the correct boxes in the grid.

Which person finds their town…

	Felix	**Lilli**	**Sophie**
Example: Small?		X	
(a) Too busy?			
(b) Good for young people?			
(c) Boring?			
(d) Noisy?			

(Total for Question 14 = 4 marks)

Where I live

A

15 Jens is talking about his home town, Duisburg.

Listen and answer the following questions in **English**.

A

(a) *Centro* is nearby. What is it? .... **(1 mark)**

(b) What has changed in the town? .... **(1 mark)**

(c) How does Jens describe the local region? .... **(1 mark)**

(d) What does Jens think of Duisburg? .... **(1 mark)**

B

(a) What does Jens say about finding a job? .... **(1 mark)**

(b) What is the problem in some districts? .... **(1 mark)**

(c) Why does he not like going to the football stadium now? .... **(1 mark)**

(d) What does Jens think he will do in the future? .... **(1 mark)**

(Total for Question 15 = 8 marks)

31

Town description

Description of a town

A*

16 Read Richard's blog about his town.

> Wir sind endlich umgezogen! Ich wohne gern hier. Die Stadt ist interessant und viel größer als Gütersloh.
>
> Ich finde es toll, dass es so viele Sportklubs, Stadien und Schwimmbäder gibt. Wir wohnen nicht weit vom neuen Freizeitzentrum entfernt, am Stadtrand.
>
> Die Stadt hat zwei sehr große Universitäten. Das ist prima, weil die Geschäfte und Cafés besonders gut für junge Leute sind. Sie sind oft viel billiger.
>
> Die Stadt ist nicht sehr modern, aber das Einkaufszentrum ist toll und es gibt mehrere Kinos und Nachtklubs. Jeden Samstag gibt es im Schlossgarten ein Konzert und ich gehe fast jede Woche dahin. Die neue Eisbahn neben dem Bahnhof ist bei Jugendlichen sehr beliebt.
>
> Viele Einwohner arbeiten in den verschiedenen Fabriken am Stadtrand, wo man zum Beispiel Autos und Flugzeuge baut. Zur Stoßzeit gibt es viel Verkehr und deshalb lange Staus.

A   What does Richard say about his town? Put a cross in the correct box.

Example: Richard findet die Stadt…

(i)	schmutzig.	
(ii)	gut.	X
(iii)	klein.	

> Pay attention to the content of the text. Don't make assumptions.

(a) Das Freizeitzentrum ist …

(i)	in der Nähe.	
(ii)	weit entfernt.	
(iii)	in der Stadtmitte.	

(c) Samstags kann man im Schlossgarten …

(i)	einen Film sehen.	
(ii)	Musik hören.	
(iii)	einkaufen.	

(b) Junge Leute können in der Stadt …

(i)	gut einkaufen.	
(ii)	nichts kaufen.	
(iii)	wenig kaufen.	

(d) Die Stadt ist …

(i)	langweilig.	
(ii)	modern.	
(iii)	industriell.	

B   Put a cross next to the **four** correct statements.

Example:	Richard wohnte einmal in einer anderen Stadt.	X
(a)	Man kann in der Stadt viel Sport treiben.	
(b)	Es gibt viele Studenten.	
(c)	Es gibt keine guten Läden für junge Leute.	
(d)	Das Stadtzentrum ist modern.	
(e)	Am Wochenende geht Richard oft in den Schlossgarten.	
(f)	Junge Leute gehen gern zur Eisbahn.	
(g)	Es gibt in der Innenstadt viel Industrie.	
(h)	Es gibt immer viel Verkehr.	

(Total for Question 16 = 8 marks)

Holiday destinations

Holiday destinations

D

17 Where do these people stay on holiday?

> **Ben:** Ich wohne am liebsten in einem Hotel in der Stadtmitte, weil es so viel zu sehen gibt. Letzten Februar waren wir in den Bergen, aber es war schrecklich.
>
> **Anna:** Jedes Jahr verbringen wir eine Woche auf einem Bauernhof auf dem Land. Ich finde das gut, weil es dort sehr ruhig ist. Ab und zu besuchen wir auch meine Oma, die in den Bergen wohnt.
>
> **Leon:** Normalerweise fahren wir an die Küste und das finde ich perfekt, besonders wenn gutes Wetter ist. Manchmal wohnen wir in einem Dorf, aber das kann total langweilig sein.

Put a cross in the correct box.

Who...

> Be careful not to focus on a single word in a sentence, as it could mislead you.

	Ben	Anna	Leon
Example: Sometimes stays in a village?			X
(a) Likes the seaside?			
(b) Likes the countryside?			
(c) Didn't like the mountains?			
(d) Stays on a farm?			

(Total for Question 17 = 4 marks)

Going on holiday

G

18 What type of holiday do these people want?

A | countryside   D | coast

B | in a town   E | mountains

C | at home   F | in a village

Listen and put a cross in the correct box.

	A	B	C	D	E	F
Example: Katharina				X		
(i) Martin						
(ii) Katja						
(iii) Max						
(iv) Ronja						

(Total for Question 18 = 4 marks)

Holiday accommodation

Holiday accommodation

B

19 Read Adam's blog about holiday accommodation.

> Jedes Jahr verbringen wir zwei Wochen in Italien. Meine Eltern wohnen am liebsten in einem Hotel. Sie wollen immer ein Zimmer mit Dusche und einem Balkon, wo sie abends sitzen können. Mein Bruder und ich haben normalerweise ein Zweibettzimmer.
>
> Viele Familien mit kleinen Kindern übernachten gern auf einem Bauernhof. Man kann natürlich im Bauernhaus schlafen, aber oft darf man dort auch zelten oder einen Wohnwagen mieten. Zelten ist billiger und es macht immer viel Spaß, draußen im Freien zu sein.
>
> Jugendherbergen sind toll für junge Leute. Normalerweise sind sie sauber und ziemlich ruhig. Sie sind bequem und haben Zimmer mit WC und Bad oder Dusche. Wenn man alleine reist, kann man oft ein Einzelzimmer buchen.

Put a cross in the correct box.

Example: Adam goes on holiday every year with …

(i)	just his brother.	
(ii)	his family.	X
(iii)	just his parents.	

(a) His parents prefer to stay in a …

(i)	youth hostel.	
(ii)	farmhouse.	
(iii)	hotel.	

(b) His parents want a room with …

(i)	a bath.	
(ii)	a balcony.	
(iii)	twin beds.	

(c) On a farm it is cheaper to stay …

(i)	in a tent.	
(ii)	in the farmhouse.	
(iii)	in a caravan.	

(d) Adam thinks youth hostels are …

(i)	comfortable.	
(ii)	dirty.	
(iii)	noisy.	

(Total for Question 19 = 4 marks)

Where do they stay?

D

20 Listen to these young people talking about their holidays. Where do they stay?
Put a cross in the correct box.

	A Bed and breakfast	B Hotel	C Caravan	D Campsite	E With a friend	F Youth hostel
Example: Ingo		X				
(i) Anja						
(ii) Nils						
(iii) Bärbel						
(iv) Max						

(Total for Question 20 = 4 marks)

Holiday homes

Advert for a flat

21 Read this advertisement for a holiday flat.

> ## Schöne Ferienwohnung im Schwarzwald
>
> Diese Ferienwohnung für sechs Personen liegt im ruhigen Schwarzwald. Sie ist im ersten Stock.
>
> Es gibt drei große Schlafzimmer, ein schönes Wohnzimmer und eine moderne Küche. Es gibt kein Esszimmer, aber das Wohnzimmer hat einen Esstisch. Das Badezimmer hat eine Dusche. Alle Schlafzimmer haben einen Kleiderschrank.
>
> Im Wohnzimmer gibt es keinen Fernsehapparat, aber im Untergeschoss kann man Tischtennis oder Billard spielen. Der Garten ist klein, aber sehr schön und wenn das Wetter gut ist, ist es toll, draußen zu essen.
>
> Der Preis ist inklusive Heizung und Bettwäsche.

What does the flat offer? Put a cross in the **four** correct boxes.

Example:	Peaceful situation	X
(a)	3 bedrooms	
(b)	Dining room	
(c)	Kitchen	
(d)	Bathroom with bath	
(e)	Bedding	
(f)	Television	
(g)	Games area	
(h)	Large garden	

> Make sure that you only cross **four** boxes.

(Total for Question 21 = 4 marks)

Holiday home

22 Frau Gottschalk is talking about a holiday home. What did she think of it?

Put a cross in the **four** correct boxes.

	Good	Bad
Example: The garden	X	
The bathrooms		
The bedrooms		
The living room		
The heating		

(Total for Question 22 = 4 marks)

35

Staying in a hotel

Staying in a hotel

E

23 Read this advertisement for a hotel.

> Das Hotel steht direkt am Marktplatz.
>
> *Zimmer:*
> Es gibt achtzehn Zimmer (Doppelzimmer, Zweibettzimmer und Einzelzimmer).
>
> Alle Zimmer haben WC und Bad.
>
> Das Restaurant ist im Erdgeschoss.
>
> *Unterhaltung:*
> • Jeden Mittwoch Kinoabend
> • Fernsehapparat im Wohnzimmer
> • Freitags Disko
>
> Leider haben wir keinen Parkplatz.

Hotel zum Markt

Answer the questions in **English**.

Example: Where is the hotel situated? ....market square..

(a) How many rooms are there? .... **(1 mark)**

(b) On which floor is the restaurant? .... **(1 mark)**

(c) What happens in the hotel on a Friday? .... **(1 mark)**

(d) What does the hotel not have? .... **(1 mark)**

(Total for Question 23 = 4 marks)

Staying in a hotel

B

24 Michelle is talking about her last holiday in a hotel.

Listen and complete the sentences by entering the correct letter.

A	a mountain view	**D**	to bed	**G**	a sea view
B	were impressed	**E**	too small	**H**	what they wanted
C	May	**F**	were disappointed	**I**	to eat

Example: The booking was made in ......C.......

(i) They booked a room with ....

(ii) When they first arrived they ....

(iii) The room was just ....

(iv) After unpacking, they went ....

(Total for Question 24 = 4 marks)

Staying at a campsite

At a campsite

D

25 Read this extract from a leaflet about a campsite.

What does the campsite offer? Put a cross in the **four** correct boxes.

Example:	Closeness to the beach	X
(a)	Camping all year	
(b)	Cheap camping	
(c)	A restaurant	
(d)	A swimming pool	
(e)	A shop	
(f)	Boat hire	
(g)	Dancing	
(h)	Cycle hire	

Zelten am Meer!

- Tolles Zelten nicht weit vom Strand – nur fünf Minuten zu Fuß.
- Wir haben nur im Winter geschlossen. (November bis März)
- Zelten ist sehr billig: €12,50 pro Nacht.
- Vor Ort finden Sie einen Laden und einen Schnellimbiss.
- Man kann viel machen:
  - im Meer schwimmen
  - am Samstagabend bis 23:00 Uhr tanzen gehen
  - in den Aufenthaltsraum gehen. (Sehr gut, wenn es regnet!)
  - Fahrräder ausleihen und die schöne Gegend sehen.
- Am Samstagvormittag gibt es in der nächsten Stadt einen großen Markt.

Guten Aufenthalt!

(Total for Question 25 = 4 marks)

My camping holidays

C

26 Emma is talking about her camping holidays. What does she like about these holidays? What does she dislike?

A	barbecue
B	the weather
C	being in a tent with her sister
D	sport
E	holidaying with her family
F	cooking
G	the restaurant

> Before you listen, try to identify what you might hear for A–G, then all you have to do when you hear the text is jot down ✓ or ✗ next to the English. Make a note too of the words that mean 'like'.
> Remember, the order will be different when you hear them!

Write the **four** correct letters in the table.

	🙂		☹
Example: C		—	

(Total for Question 26 = 4 marks)

37

Holiday preferences

Holiday choices

C

27 Read what these teenagers wrote.

> **A:** Ich mache lieber Urlaub in der Nähe vom Meer, wo ich den ganzen Tag am Strand liegen kann.
>
> **B:** Zelten auf dem Land ist prima, besonders wenn es auf dem Campingplatz ein Schwimmbad gibt.
>
> **C:** Das kleine Hotel in Italien war super für die ganze Familie.
>
> **D:** Sieben Nächte auf einem Schiff auf der Donau. Fantastisch! Es ist ganz ruhig auf dem Fluss.
>
> **E:** Eine Jugendherberge auf dem Land ist toll, wenn man mit ein paar Freunden Urlaub macht.
>
> **F:** Ich wohne lieber in einem Hotel in der Stadtmitte, weil ich gerne interessante Museen und Schlösser besuche.

Who mentions which type of holiday? Write the correct letter in the boxes.

Example:	A quiet holiday	D
(i)	A sightseeing holiday	
(ii)	A camping holiday	
(iii)	A group holiday	
(iv)	A beach holiday	

(Total for Question 27 = 4 marks)

Holiday activities

C

28 Listen to these girls talking about what they like to do on holiday.

Who says what? Write the correct letter in the boxes.

A I like to relax.	**D** I go shopping.
B I like the night life.	**E** I do lots of sports.
C I get up late.	**F** I want to see all the sights.

	Patricia	Manuela
Example:	B	–

(Total for Question 28 = 4 marks)

Holiday activities

Holiday activities

29 You read part of an online discussion about holiday activities.

Hannah (18) aus Hamburg schreibt:

Jeder freut sich auf den Sommerurlaub. Man will sich ein paar Wochen gut amüsieren und ausruhen.

Meine Freunde fahren lieber ohne Eltern weg. Sie reisen zum Beispiel ins Ausland, weil sie das wärmere Wetter lieben. Sie bleiben meistens an der Küste. Sie können dann den ganzen Tag schwimmen, am Strand liegen und Volleyball oder Fußball spielen.

Abends ist viel los. Sie tanzen bis spät in die Nacht oder unterhalten sich in Cafés und Lokalen. Weil sie so spät ins Bett gehen, stehen sie gewöhnlich vormittags nicht sehr früh auf.

Normalerweise besuchen sie nicht gern historische Sehenswürdigkeiten wie Burgen oder alte Kirchen, weil sie das zu langweilig finden.

Answer the questions in **English**. You do not need to write in full sentences.

(a) What does Hannah say people want to do on holiday? Give **one** example.

.... (1 mark)

(b) Why do her friends like to go abroad?

.... (1 mark)

(c) Where do they usually stay?

.... (1 mark)

(d) What can they do all day? Give **two** examples.

(i) .... (1 mark)

(ii) .... (1 mark)

(e) Why do they usually get up quite late?

.... (1 mark)

(f) What **don't** they want to do?

.... (1 mark)

(g) Why don't they want to do that?

.... (1 mark)

(Total for Question 29 = 8 marks)

Booking accommodation

 Booking accommodation

E   **30** Max sends an email to the manager of a youth hostel.

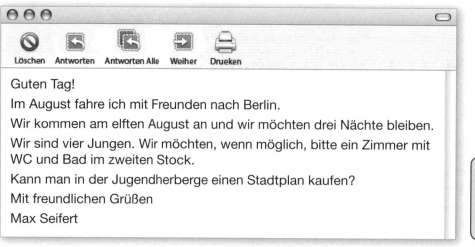

Löschen   Antworten   Antworten Alle   Weiher   Drueken

Guten Tag!

Im August fahre ich mit Freunden nach Berlin.

Wir kommen am elften August an und wir möchten drei Nächte bleiben.

Wir sind vier Jungen. Wir möchten, wenn möglich, bitte ein Zimmer mit WC und Bad im zweiten Stock.

Kann man in der Jugendherberge einen Stadtplan kaufen?

Mit freundlichen Grüßen

Max Seifert

> Remember to write in **English**. You will not gain any marks for German answers.

Answer the questions in **English**. Full sentences are not needed.

Example: Where is Max going? ..... Berlin .....

(a) On what date will Max and his friends arrive? .... **(1 mark)**

(b) How many people is he booking for? .... **(1 mark)**

(c) What does he ask for in the bathroom? Toilet and .... **(1 mark)**

(d) What does he want to buy in the youth hostel? .... **(1 mark)**

(Total for Question 30 = 4 marks)

 Booking a room in a hotel

B   **31** Annett is booking into a hotel. Put a cross next to the correct answer.

Example: She is staying…

(i)	one day.	
(ii)	two days.	X
(iii)	a few days.	

(a) She is leaving the hotel on the…

(i)	5th August.	
(ii)	14th August.	
(iii)	15th August.	

(b) She asks for a room with…

(i)	a sea view.	
(ii)	a balcony.	
(iii)	a television.	

(c) Breakfast…

(i)	is included.	
(ii)	costs extra.	
(iii)	is not provided.	

(d) She also asks for…

(i)	internet access.	
(ii)	half board.	
(iii)	a morning paper.	

(Total for Question 31 = 4 marks)

Future holiday plans

Alexander's holiday plans

B 32 Read Alexander's letter.

> Lieber Opa,
>
> vielen Dank für das Geld. Es ist sehr nützlich, weil ich für den Urlaub einen besseren Rucksack brauche. Ich werde mit meinem Freund Markus durch Frankreich und Spanien reisen.
>
> Am vierten September fahren wir los. Ich bin schon sehr gespannt! Markus hat ein Motorrad und die Reise wird viel Spaß machen. Wenn das Geld reicht, bleiben wir vier Wochen weg.
>
> Obwohl wir meistens zelten werden, wollen wir ab und zu auch in kleinen Hotels wohnen. Dann werden wir abends in einem billigen Restaurant essen.
>
> Wir werden in einigen Städten ein bisschen länger bleiben, um die besten Sehenswürdigkeiten zu besuchen.
>
> Ich schicke Dir viele Postkarten!
>
> Viele Grüße von Alexander

Put a cross next to the **four** correct statements about Alexander.

Example:	He is writing to his grandfather.	X
(a)	He had a rucksack from his grandfather.	
(b)	He plans to travel outside Germany.	
(c)	He hopes to be away two months.	
(d)	He will use his friend's transport.	
(e)	He will always stay on a campsite.	
(f)	He will vary how long he stays in places.	
(g)	He will do some sightseeing.	
(h)	He will email his grandfather.	

(Total for Question 32 = 4 marks)

Holiday plans

A* 33 Cem is asking Verena what she wants to do on holiday.

Which statements are correct? Listen and put a cross against the **four** correct answers.

(a)	She has already visited Italy.	
(b)	She is attracted by the Italian scenery.	
(c)	She prefers going on holiday alone.	
(d)	Her friend Bettina is going to America in September.	
(e)	Verena's visit to America will be a family holiday.	
(f)	In America, she could rent a car.	
(g)	Next year she's going to Switzerland to ski.	
(h)	Verena loves hiking.	

(Total for Question 33 = 4 marks)

Past holidays

A holiday report

A* 34 Read Leah's holiday report.

> Die Reise im letzten August zum Bodensee war ziemlich lang, aber mein Vater hatte alles gut geplant. Unser Auto ist alt und wir haben regelmäßig an Raststätten auf der Autobahn gehalten.
>
> Meine Eltern hatten eine kleine Wohnung mit einer schönen Aussicht auf den See gemietet. Die Unterkunft war besser, als sie erwartet hatten.
>
> Das Wetter war wechselhaft, aber es hat nicht zu viel geregnet. Der Tagesausflug mit der Fähre in die Schweiz war sehr schön, weil es den ganzen Tag sonnig war. Wir haben auch einige interessante Schlösser in der Umgebung besucht. Die kleinen Städte waren hübsch und sehr sauber, aber die Straßen waren steil und sehr eng. Es gab viele Touristen und es war schwer zu laufen.
>
> Es war ein toller Sommerurlaub. Nächstes Jahr will ich unbedingt noch einmal dorthin fahren, obwohl meine Familie nach Spanien fährt. Ich würde lieber mit Freunden Urlaub am Bodensee machen und nicht ins Ausland reisen.

What does Leah say about the holiday? Put a cross in the correct box.

Example: Leah beschreibt…

(i)	einen Urlaub mit Freunden.	
(ii)	einen Winterurlaub.	
(iii)	einen Familienurlaub.	X

(a) Der Urlaub war…

(i)	im April.	
(ii)	vor zwei Jahren.	
(iii)	letztes Jahr.	

(b) Leahs Vater hat…

(i)	ein Auto gemietet.	
(ii)	die Fahrt organisiert.	
(iii)	unterwegs nicht gehalten.	

(c) Die Wohnung war…

(i)	sehr gut.	
(ii)	nicht gut.	
(iii)	zu klein.	

(d) Das Wetter war…

(i)	schlecht.	
(ii)	immer regnerisch.	
(iii)	manchmal gut.	

(e) Sie sind an einem Tag…

(i)	mit dem Schiff gefahren.	
(ii)	Rad gefahren.	
(iii)	mit dem Reisebus gefahren.	

(f) In der Gegend gab es…

(i)	nichts zu sehen.	
(ii)	schöne Sehenswürdigkeiten.	
(iii)	nicht viel zu tun.	

(g) Die Straßen waren…

(i)	schmutzig.	
(ii)	flach.	
(iii)	nicht breit.	

(h) Nächstes Jahr will sie…

(i)	nach Spanien fahren.	
(ii)	wieder zum Bodensee fahren.	
(iii)	mit ihren Eltern wegfahren.	

(Total for Question 34 = 8 marks)

Directions

Directions

C

35 Read these directions.

A	„Geh geradeaus bis zur Bibliothek."
B	„Geh über die Kreuzung und nimm die dritte Straße links."
C	„Nimm die nächste Straße rechts und geh geradeaus."
D	„Geh an der Ampel nach rechts."
E	„Geh links am Krankenhaus vorbei. Der Park ist auf der rechten Seite."
F	„Geh über die Brücke und nimm die zweite Straße rechts."
G	„An der Ecke ist die Bank. Geh an der Bank nach rechts."
H	„Geh über den Platz und nimm die zweite Straße links."

Which direction is it? Write the correct letter in each box.

Example:	Go left at the hospital.	E
(i)	Go over the bridge and take the second right.	
(ii)	Go right at the traffic lights.	
(iii)	Go straight on to the library.	
(iv)	Go right at the bank.	

(Total for Question 35 = 4 marks)

Getting to school

F

36 Which way do these people go to get to school?

A	right at the crossroads	**D**	past the town hall
B	round the corner	**E**	straight on
C	left	**F**	over the bridge

Listen and put a cross in the correct box.

	A	**B**	**C**	**D**	**E**	**F**
Example:					X	
(i)						
(ii)						
(iii)						
(iv)						

(Total for Question 36 = 4 marks)

Travelling

 Transport

F **37** How do these people travel?

A „Ich fahre gern mit dem Boot auf dem Bodensee."

B „Ich fahre mit dem Bus in die Stadt."

C „Alex fährt jeden Tag mit dem Mofa."

D „Ich fliege mit dem Flugzeug nach Berlin."

E „Paul fährt mit dem Auto zum Stadion."

F „In London fährt man mit der U-Bahn."

Write the correct letter.

Example:	By bus	B
(i)	By underground	
(ii)	By boat	
(iii)	By car	
(iv)	By moped	

(Total for Question 37 = 4 marks)

 Getting around

D **38** Michael is talking about the ways he travels.

Listen and put a cross in the correct box.

Which form of transport does Michael use to go to …

> Look at the transport options A–F and think of the German words before you listen.

	A on foot	**B** by moped	**C** by tram	**D** by train	**E** by bike	**F** by car
Example: the swimming pool?					X	
(i) school?						
(ii) meet friends?						
(iii) Salzburg?						
(iv) his girlfriend's?						

(Total for Question 38 = 4 marks)

Transport

Opinions on transport

Ⓒ   **39** Read what Sara says about transport.

> Man sollte am besten mit öffentlichen Verkehrsmitteln fahren. Aber wir wohnen in einem Dorf und brauchen deshalb ein Auto. Oft fährt nur ein Bus pro Tag vom Dorf in die Stadtmitte, und eine Rückfahrkarte kostet sehr viel.
>
> Weil es in der Stadtmitte oft Staus gibt, fahren viele Leute lieber mit der Straßenbahn. Die Straßenbahnen sind pünktlich und die Fahrkarten sind billig.
>
> Ich fand die U-Bahn in Berlin toll. Man kann so schnell in der Stadt herumfahren, aber es gibt immer sehr viele Leute und es ist sehr laut.

> Don't be misled by picking the first word you recognise. Look at all the choices.

Complete the information by choosing the correct letter.

A late	**D** public transport	**G** a car
B every day	**E** noisy	**H** quiet
C cheap	**F** on time	**I** expensive

Example: People should use ......D........ .

(i) Return bus tickets are ....

(ii) Trams run ....

(iii) Tram tickets are ....

(iv) The underground is ....

(Total for Question 39 = 4 marks)

Getting around

Ⓐ*   **40** Julia is talking about travel.

Complete the sentences by putting a cross in the correct box.

Example: Julia never travels by…

(i)	bus.	X
(ii)	car.	
(iii)	train.	

(a) For Julia, travelling by car is…

(i)	quicker.	
(ii)	cheaper.	
(iii)	safer.	

(b) At the airport, she does not like waiting…

(i)	in the lounge.	
(ii)	to eat.	
(iii)	at the check-in.	

(c) She walks to school because she…

(i)	has no bike.	
(ii)	does not like traffic.	
(iii)	likes running.	

(d) She travels by train…

(i)	a lot.	
(ii)	whenever possible.	
(iii)	hardly ever.	

(Total for Question 40 = 4 marks)

At the café

In a café

G

1 Read the meal order for table 7.

Café am Dom

Tisch 7:
Hähnchen
Pommes frites
Eis
Saft
Kaffee

What did the customer order? Put a cross in the other **four** correct boxes.

Example: A ☒

B ☐

C ☐

D ☐

E ☐

F ☐

G ☐

H ☐

I ☐

(Total for Question 1 = 4 marks)

39 Eating in a café

F

2 What do these people order? Put a cross in the correct space.

	A Salad	B Chips	C Fruit juice	D Omelette	E Ice cream	F Sausage
Example:	X					
(i)						
(ii)						
(iii)						
(iv)						

(Total for Question 2 = 4 marks)

Eating in a café

 A new café

E 3 You read this article about a new café.

> Café Max ist ein neues Café am Markt. Die Kellner sind alle sehr freundlich und das Café ist toll für junge Leute.
>
> Das Essen schmeckt sehr gut. Es gibt alles und das Eis ist fantastisch. Mein Lieblingseis ist Himbeereis. Leider ist der Kaffee ziemlich teuer.

Answer the questions in **English.**

(a) What are the waiters like?

.... **(1 mark)**

(b) What sort of people would find the café great?

.... **(1 mark)**

(c) What does the writer think of the ice cream?

.... **(1 mark)**

(d) What is said about the coffee?

.... **(1 mark)**

(Total for Question 3 = 4 marks)

 Eating out

C 4 Susanne and Michael give their opinions on eating out.

Who says what? Listen and put a cross in the **four** correct boxes.

		Susanne	Michael
Example:	I prefer a restaurant.	X	
(a)	The choice is not so good in self-service.		
(b)	In a restaurant you wait too long to eat.		
(c)	Fast food is cheap.		
(d)	Fast food is not good for you.		
(e)	It's good to have a waiter serve you.		

(Total for Question 4 = 4 marks)

At a coffee house

Coffee shops

C 5 You read these opinions on coffee shops.

Johannes: Ich gehe gern mit Freunden ins Kaffeehaus. Es macht Spaß, Kaffee zu trinken und stundenlang zu plaudern.

Anna: Es ist nicht billig, ins Kaffeehaus zu gehen, besonders wenn man auch ein Stück Torte bestellt.

Leah: In unserer Stadt gibt es viele tolle Kaffeehäuser. Man muss nicht weit laufen, um einen wunderbaren Kaffee zu finden.

Hasan: Ich trinke nicht gern Kaffee oder Tee, aber ich liebe Kakao mit Sahne!

Daniel: Ich gehe nicht gern in Kaffeehäuser, weil sie oft nicht sauber sind.

Tom: Es gibt immer zu viele Leute in den Kaffeehäusern in der Stadtmitte. Man muss zu lange warten.

Put a cross in the **four** correct boxes.

Who finds coffee shops …

	Johannes	Anna	Leah	Hasan	Daniel	Tom
Example: convenient?			X			
(a) dirty?						
(b) sociable?						
(c) crowded?						
(d) expensive?						

(Total for Question 5 = 4 marks)

41 **At the coffee house**

G 6 What do these people order at the coffee house?

Put a cross in the correct box.

	A	B	C	D	E	F
Example:		X				
(i)						
(ii)						
(iii)						
(iv)						

(Total for Question 6 = 4 marks)

At a restaurant

Eating in a restaurant

C

7   Read Hanna's blog.

> Einmal im Monat geht die ganze Familie ins Restaurant. Wir machen das sehr gerne.
>
> Normalerweise gehen wir in ein kleines Restaurant in der Nähe, das wir alle lieben. Die Kellner sind sehr freundlich und das Essen ist fantastisch.
>
> Es gibt verschiedene Spezialitäten aus vielen Ländern, aber ich liebe Schnitzel mit Kartoffeln und Salat. Meine Mutter ist Vegetarierin und isst oft Nudeln mit einer schmackhaften Tomatensoße. Wir essen keine Vorspeise, aber wir bestellen immer einen Nachtisch! Die Schokoladentorte ist besonders gut!

Put a cross next to the **four** correct statements.

Example:	Hanna's family goes to the restaurant once a month.	X
(a)	The restaurant is quite far away.	
(b)	The waiters are friendly.	
(c)	The food is quite good.	
(d)	They serve food from different countries.	
(e)	Hanna loves the pasta.	
(f)	Hanna's mother doesn't eat meat.	
(g)	They always have a starter.	
(h)	Hanna likes the chocolate gateau.	

(Total for Question 7 = 4 marks)

At a restaurant

B

8   Matthias und Eva have just finished their meal at a restaurant.
Listen and put a cross to show what each person liked.

	Matthias	**Eva**
Example: Starter	X	
Fish		
Pork chop		
Dessert		
Drinks		

(Total for Question 8 = 4 marks)

Opinions about food

Opinions about food

D   9   You read these comments.

Sara:	Nudeln sind leicht zu kochen und sie sind sehr lecker.
Ben:	Als Nachspeise esse ich lieber Obst, weil es gesund ist.
Ali:	Fettiges Essen wie Pommes schmeckt mir gut, aber es ist nicht gesund.
Leila:	Ich finde Fisch schmackhaft, aber ich esse lieber Fleisch.
Jacob:	Nachspeisen schmecken mir nicht, wenn sie zu süß sind.
Adam:	Weil es mir zu kalt ist, kann ich kein Eis essen.

Which person is this? Put a cross in the correct box.

	Sara	Ben	Ali	Leila	Jacob	Adam
Example: Likes pasta.	X					
(a) Likes some unhealthy foods.						
(b) Can't eat ice cream.						
(c) Prefers meat.						
(d) Dislikes very sweet desserts.						

(Total for Question 9 = 4 marks)

Opinions about food

C   10 Markus and Anke are looking at the menu in a restaurant. What do they say?

Put a cross in the correct box.

Example: Anke…

(i)	likes tomatoes.	
(ii)	does not like tomatoes.	X
(iii)	likes only tomato soup.	

(a) Anke wants…

(i)	tomato soup.	
(ii)	chicken soup.	
(iii)	no soup.	

(b) Markus wants…

(i)	a hamburger.	
(ii)	fish.	
(iii)	chicken.	

(c) Anke chooses a salad because she…

(i)	wants to stay slim.	
(ii)	is a vegetarian.	
(iii)	thinks it is healthy.	

(d) Anke thinks that what Markus eats…

(i)	tastes great.	
(ii)	will make him fat.	
(iii)	is very healthy.	

(Total for Question 10 = 4 marks)

Restaurant problems

Complaining about a restaurant

11 Read Sara's email to the manager of a restaurant.

Löschen   Antworten   Antworten Alle   Weiher   Drueken

Gestern Abend war ich mit meiner Familie in Ihrem Restaurant, um den Geburtstag meiner Mutter zu feiern. Mein Vater hatte vor einem Monat einen Tisch reserviert, weil wir neben dem Fenster sitzen wollten.

Wir sind rechtzeitig um 19:30 Uhr angekommen, aber wir mussten eine halbe Stunde auf einen Tisch warten. Ich war so enttäuscht*, als ich den Tisch gesehen habe. Er war gleich neben den Toiletten! Die Kellnerin war sehr nett, aber das Restaurant war voll und sie konnte keinen anderen Tisch finden.

Obwohl die Vorspeisen und Fleischgerichte ziemlich gut geschmeckt haben, waren die vegetarischen Hauptgerichte kalt. Außerdem war wenig Obst auf der Obsttorte.

Es war ein furchtbares Erlebnis und ich werde nie wieder in Ihr Restaurant gehen.

Sara Fischer

* disappointed

Answer the questions in **English.** You do not need to write in sentences.

> Keep your answers short.

(a) When was the visit to the restaurant?

.... **(1 mark)**

(b) What were they celebrating?

.... **(1 mark)**

(c) When had Sara's father booked the table?

.... **(1 mark)**

(d) Why was Sara disappointed when she saw where the table was?

.... **(1 mark)**

(e) What couldn't the waitress do for them?

.... **(1 mark)**

(f) What was the problem with the food?

(i) .... **(1 mark)**

(ii) .... **(1 mark)**

(g) What is Sara **not** going to do?

.... **(1 mark)**

(Total for Question 11 = 8 marks)

Had a go ☐   Nearly there ☐   Nailed it! ☐

Shops

 Shops

G 12 Look at these types of shops.

A	Metzgerei	D	Apotheke
B	Post	E	Gemüseladen
C	Bäckerei	F	Warenhaus

Which shop is it?

Example:	Greengrocer's shop	E
(i)	Baker's shop	
(ii)	Butcher's shop	
(iii)	Department store	
(iv)	Chemist	

(Total for Question 12 = 4 marks)

 Favourite shops

A 13 Two people are talking about their favourite type of shop. Answer the following questions.

    A Leon

    (a) Why did he need to go to his favourite shop last week?

    .... **(1 mark)**

    (b) What **two** reasons does he give for shopping there?

        (i) .... **(1 mark)**

        (ii) .... **(1 mark)**

    (c) What else did he buy while he was there? .... **(1 mark)**

    B Maria

    (a) Why does she have so many clothes?

    .... **(1 mark)**

    (b) What does she do when she walks into the shop?

    .... **(1 mark)**

    (c) What does she enjoy doing?

    .... **(1 mark)**

    (d) When does she go to the hairdresser?

    .... **(1 mark)**

(Total for Question 13 = 8 marks)

At the market

Anna goes shopping

14 Anna's mother has left this note.

> Anna, kannst du heute bitte zum Markt gehen?
>
> Wir brauchen zwei Gurken für den Gurkensalat und ein Kilo Kartoffeln für den Kartoffelsalat. Kannst du bitte kleine Kartoffeln kaufen?
>
> Ich möchte für morgen auch einen Blumenkohl.
>
> Zum Nachtisch können wir heute Obst essen. Kannst du also bitte ein Kilo Erdbeeren kaufen?
>
> Danke.
>
> Mama

Answer the questions in **English.**

Example: How many cucumbers must Anna buy? ......2......

(a) How many potatoes must Anna buy? .... **(1 mark)**

(b) What should the potatoes be like? .... **(1 mark)**

(c) What must she buy for tomorrow? .... **(1 mark)**

(d) What must she buy for dessert? .... **(1 mark)**

(Total for Question 14 = 4 marks)

At the market

15 Ronja is shopping at the market. Listen and answer the following questions in **English.**

(a) What does Ronja buy after the cabbage? .... **(1 mark)**

(b) What does she want next? .... **(1 mark)**

(c) What does an orange cost? .... **(1 mark)**

(d) How many raspberries does she buy? .... **(1 mark)**

(Total for Question 15 = 4 marks)

Shopping for food

Shopping list

F 16 Read Meryem's shopping list.

Which items are on Meryem's list?
Put a cross in the **four** correct boxes.

Example:	Peas	X
(a)	Strawberry jam	
(b)	Chocolate	
(c)	Coffee	
(d)	Loaf of bread	
(e)	Bread rolls	
(f)	Mushrooms	
(g)	Apples	
(h)	Ham	

EINKAUFSLISTE

Supermarkt:
eine kleine Dose Erbsen
ein Glas Himbeermarmelade
eine Tafel Schokolade für Mama
eine Packung Tee

Bäckerei:
6 Brötchen für das Frühstück

Markt:
8 große Tomaten
kleine Pilze für die Pizza
4 rote Apfelsinen

Metzger:
3 dünne Scheiben Schinken
1 großes Hähnchen für Sonntag

(Total for Question 16 = 4 marks)

Food shopping

A* 17 Caro has been shopping with Paul. Listen and put a cross in the correct box.

Example: Paul is…

(i)	her friend.	
(ii)	her brother.	X
(iii)	her cousin.	

(a) Caro thought shopping with Paul was…

(i)	fun.	
(ii)	awful.	
(iii)	exciting.	

(b) Paul wanted to buy…

(i)	sweet things.	
(ii)	ham.	
(iii)	cheese.	

(c) Caro's mother gets upset if Caro…

(i)	forgets something.	
(ii)	goes shopping without Paul.	
(iii)	buys something not on the list.	

(d) Caro bought chewing gum…

(i)	to be nice to Paul.	
(ii)	to keep Paul quiet.	
(iii)	with Paul's money.	

(Total for Question 17 = 4 marks)

Shopping

Ahmed's blog

C

18 Read Ahmed's blog.

> Ich gehe gern einkaufen. Letzte Woche habe ich im Schaufenster eines Kaufhauses einen tollen MP3-Spieler gesehen. Im Moment spare ich und ich hoffe, ihn nächsten Monat zu kaufen.
>
> Jeden Freitag gehe ich mit meinem Vater in den Supermarkt. Ich finde es nicht zu langweilig, aber letzten Freitag war es furchtbar, weil der Einkaufswagen kaputt war!
>
> Ich kaufe gern Kleidung auf dem Markt, weil es dort oft billiger als im Kaufhaus ist. Letzten Samstag habe ich eine tolle Hose gefunden und sie hat nicht viel gekostet.
>
> Am Wochenende werde ich mit meinem Vater einkaufen gehen, um einen neuen Fernsehapparat zu suchen.

Do these activities belong in the past, present or future? Put a cross in the correct box.

> Look for time phrases as well as key verbs and signs of tenses.

		Past	Present	Future
Example:	Saving for an MP3 player		X	
(a)	Buying an MP3 player			
(b)	Having a broken shopping trolley			
(c)	Finding a pair of trousers			
(d)	Looking for a new TV			

(Total for Question 18 = 4 marks)

Buying a present

B

19 Patricia is shopping for a present for her niece. Listen and put a cross in the correct box.

Example: Patricia's niece is…

(i)	13.	
(ii)	14.	X
(iii)	15.	

(a) Patricia rejects the handbag because…

(i)	her niece is too young.	
(ii)	it is old fashioned.	
(iii)	it is too expensive.	

(c) Patricia's niece wears…

(i)	earrings.	
(ii)	necklaces.	
(iii)	no jewellery.	

(b) Patricia doesn't want lipstick because…

(i)	her niece is too young for it.	
(ii)	her niece never wears make-up.	
(iii)	it isn't the right colour.	

(d) Patricia decides to buy…

(i)	make-up.	
(ii)	jewellery.	
(iii)	perfume.	

(Total for Question 19 = 4 marks)

Shop signs

 Signs in shops

D 20 You see these shop signs.

A

Tolle
Sonderangebote
heute in der
Damenabteilung!

Bis **50%** Rabatt.

B

Neues Elektrogeschäft
im ersten Stock.

C

Öffnungszeiten:
Mo.–Fr.: 08:30–18:00 Uhr
Sa.: 08:30–14:00 Uhr
Sonntags geschlossen

D

Bitte behalten Sie Ihre
Quittung, sonst können
Sie die Waren nicht
umtauschen.

E

Wenn Sie die
Umkleidekabinen brauchen,
warten Sie bitte auf eine
Verkäuferin.

F

Bitte zahlen Sie an
der Kasse neben
dem Ausgang.

Which sign is it? Write the correct letter in the box.

Example:	Opening times	C
(i)	Changing rooms	
(ii)	Reductions	
(iii)	Where to pay	
(iv)	Keeping receipts	

(Total for Question 20 = 4 marks)

48 **Saskia's shopping trip**

C 21 Saskia has been shopping. Listen and put a cross in the correct box.

Example: Saskia was at the…

(i)	town centre.	
(ii)	shopping centre.	X
(iii)	market.	

(a) The opening times are…

(i)	10 a.m – 8 p.m.	
(ii)	9 a.m. – 9 p.m.	
(iii)	11 a.m. – 9 p.m.	

(b) She found that…

(i)	the shops were closed.	
(ii)	the escalator was broken.	
(iii)	the lift was out of order.	

(c) It was busy because…

(i)	of the special offers this week.	
(ii)	it was the winter sale.	
(iii)	it was the summer sale.	

(d) She was disappointed because…

(i)	she did not like the clothes they had.	
(ii)	what she wanted was sold out.	
(iii)	the clothes were too dear.	

(Total for Question 21 = 4 marks)

Clothes and colours

Shopping for clothes

F 22 These people are shopping for clothes.

A „Haben Sie eine rote Hose, bitte?"

B „Ich möchte bitte einen grünen Rock."

C „Ich suche bitte einen blauen Pulli."

D „Ich möchte eine gelbe Badehose."

E „Ich mag das graue Kleid nicht."

F „Ich finde die schwarze Jacke toll."

Which clothes are mentioned? Write the correct letter in each box.

Example:	Blue jumper	C
(i)	Grey dress	
(ii)	Red trousers	
(iii)	Black jacket	
(iv)	Green skirt	

(Total for Question 22 = 4 marks)

At the clothes shop

F 23 What clothes does the shop have? Listen and put a cross in the correct space.

	A Dress	B Trousers	C Skirt	D Pullover	E Shoes	F Shirt
Example:	X					
(i)						
(ii)						
(iii)						
(iv)						

(Total for Question 23 = 4 marks)

Had a go ☐   Nearly there ☐   Nailed it! ☐

Buying clothes

Buying clothes

C   24 Read what these teenagers say about buying clothes.

A   „Die Farbe muss mir gut stehen. Das ist sehr wichtig für mich."

B   „Ich probiere Klamotten zu Hause an, weil die Umkleidekabinen im Laden viel zu eng sind."

C   „Ich liebe Mode und ich kaufe jeden Monat neue Klamotten."

D   „Eine Hose muss lang genug sein. Wenn sie zu kurz ist, kaufe ich sie nicht."

E   „Ich kaufe Klamotten auf dem Markt, weil sie viel billiger sind."

F   „Ich kaufe lieber Kleidung aus Baumwolle, weil sie bequemer als Kleidung aus Wolle ist."

Who mentions what? Write the correct letter in the box.

Example:	Colour	A
(i)	Length	
(ii)	Price	
(iii)	Trying on	
(iv)	Fabric	

(Total for Question 24 = 4 marks)

Katharina's choices

D   25 Katharina is shopping for clothes with her friend, Anja. Listen. What does she say about each of Anja's suggestions?

Make sure you only put four **crosses**.

	A Skirt	B Blouse	C Jeans	D Dress
Example: Too short	X			
(i) Not fashionable				
(ii) Not her size				
(iii) Too old for her				
(iv) Too expensive				

(Total for Question 25 = 4 marks)

Returning clothes

Returning clothes

B

26 Read the reasons customers have given for returning goods.

A „Ich habe die Schuhe letzte Woche gekauft, aber sie passen nicht zum Kleid. Die Farbe ist zu hell."

B „Als ich die Strickjacke heute anziehen wollte, habe ich ein großes Loch im Ärmel gefunden."

C „Ich habe die Hose online gekauft – sie sollte aus Wolle sein, aber sie ist aus Kunststoff."

D „Obwohl das Kleid sehr schön ist, passt es mir nicht gut. Es ist ein bisschen zu eng."

E „Die Hose passt mir sehr gut, aber meine Mutter findet sie zu teuer. Ich möchte bitte mein Geld zurück."

F „Ich möchte die Jacke umtauschen, weil sie zu warm für den Sommer ist."

Why have the items been returned? Write the correct letter in the box.

Example:	Colour	A
(i)	Fabric	
(ii)	Damaged	
(iii)	Size	
(iv)	Suitability	

(Total for Question 26 = 4 marks)

Returning an item

E

27 Julian is returning an item of clothing to the shop. Listen and complete the sentences with a word or phrase from the list.

A a present	**D** a size smaller	**G** one in blue
B one in red	**E** not to take it	**H** more
C to take it	**F** less	**I** a size bigger

Example: The pullover was .... A ....

(i) Julian asks for ....

(ii) The shop has only ....

(iii) Julian decides ....

(iv) It costs ....

(Total for Question 27 = 4 marks)

Online shopping

Shopping online

A

28 You read an article about online shopping.

> Immer mehr Leute kaufen online, weil es praktisch und oft billiger ist. Aber der größte Vorteil ist, dass es so viele verschiedene Produkte gibt.
>
> Das Internet ist besonders gut, wenn man zum Beispiel interessante Geschenke für Familie und Freunde sucht. Es gibt Hunderte Ideen und man kann gute Marken zu tollen Preisen kaufen.
>
> Viele Leute benutzen das Internet, um Klamotten zu kaufen. Der Nachteil ist, dass man die Kleidung nicht anprobieren kann, bevor man sie kauft. Manche Leute gehen lieber in einen Laden, um sich die Sachen genau anzusehen. Dann kaufen sie die Waren preiswerter online.
>
> Es ist möglich, viel Zeit zu sparen, wenn man Supermarkteinkäufe online macht. Es ist prima, weil man alles machen kann, ohne das Haus zu verlassen. Leider gibt es manchmal auch Probleme. So kann es vorkommen, dass die Einkäufe sehr spät kommen oder das Obst und Gemüse nicht frisch sind.

> You do not need to write in sentences.
> Often two or three words will be enough.

Answer the questions in **English.**

(a) What is the main advantage of online shopping?

.... **(1 mark)**

(b) Why is the internet good for presents?

(i) .... **(1 mark)**

(ii) .... **(1 mark)**

(c) What is the disadvantage of buying clothes online?

.... **(1 mark)**

(d) What do some people do before buying online?

.... **(1 mark)**

(e) Why is online supermarket shopping good?

(i) .... **(1 mark)**

(ii) .... **(1 mark)**

(f) Give **one** example of a problem with online supermarket shopping.

.... **(1 mark)**

(Total for Question 28 = 8 marks)

Opinions about shopping

Shopping preferences

Ⓐ* **29** You read the following article.

> Am Wochenende sind Einkaufszentren und Stadtzentren überfüllt. Einkaufen scheint als Freizeitaktivität beliebter als Joggen oder Schwimmen zu sein.
>
> Jeden Samstag schaut sich **Max (16)** in den Geschäften in der Stadtmitte um. Er kauft nur ab und zu etwas, aber er findet es toll, sich am Wochenende die neueste Mode anzusehen. Er geht lieber mit Freunden einkaufen. „Ich probiere etwas an. Dann helfen sie mir, wenn ich nicht weiß, ob ich es kaufen soll. Leider bezahlen sie nicht!"

> **Anna (15)** kann Einkaufen nicht leiden. „Einkaufen interessiert mich gar nicht. Ich treibe lieber Sport. Meine Mutter kauft meine Klamotten im Internet. Ich finde das praktisch, weil ich alles zu Hause anprobieren kann. Es ist auch einfach und billiger."
>
> Für **Maria (18)** ist Mode ihre große Leidenschaft. Sie findet Mode viel besser als Sport oder Musik. „Ich gehe lieber in Boutiquen, weil die Kleidung dort besonders modisch ist. Die Auswahl ist vielleicht nicht so groß wie in größeren Geschäften und Warenhäusern, aber man findet schöne Sachen, die ein bisschen anders und nicht zu teuer sind."

What is said about shopping? Put a cross in the correct box.

Example: Am Wochenende gehen viele Leute lieber…

(i)	einkaufen.	X
(ii)	joggen.	
(iii)	schwimmen.	

(a) Max kauft … etwas.

(i)	jedes Wochenende	
(ii)	jeden Samstag	
(iii)	manchmal	

(b) Max interessiert sich für…

(i)	modische Kleidung.	
(ii)	billige Kleidung.	
(iii)	teure Kleidung.	

(c) Seine Freunde helfen ihm,…

(i)	zu entscheiden.	
(ii)	zu bezahlen.	
(iii)	Kleidung anzuprobieren.	

(d) Anna mag Einkaufen…

(i)	nicht besonders.	
(ii)	mit ihrer Mutter.	
(iii)	überhaupt nicht.	

(e) Sie findet online Einkaufen…

(i)	kompliziert.	
(ii)	teuer.	
(iii)	nützlich.	

(f) Maria ist…

(i)	Modefanatikerin.	
(ii)	Sportfanatikerin.	
(iii)	Musikfanatikerin.	

(g) Sie geht lieber in…

(i)	kleinere Geschäfte.	
(ii)	größere Geschäfte.	
(iii)	Kaufhäuser.	

(h) Klamotten in Boutiquen sind…

(i)	immer das Gleiche.	
(ii)	teuer.	
(iii)	nicht das Gleiche.	

(Total for Question 29 = 8 marks)

Emergency services

An accident

C   **30** You read this report.

> Gestern Abend gab es zwischen Köln und Bonn einen Verkehrsunfall. Jemand hat sofort 112 gewählt und eine halbe Stunde später sind die Polizei und ein Krankenwagen angekommen.
>
> Vier Menschen mussten ins Krankenhaus nach Köln gebracht werden. Ein Mann und eine Frau konnten heute früh nach Hause gehen, aber zwei Frauen müssen länger im Krankenhaus bleiben.
>
> Die Polizei möchte mehr Informationen über den Unfall haben. Wer den Unfall gesehen hat, sollte bitte die Polizei in Bonn anrufen.

Complete the information by choosing the correct letter.

A	in hospital	**D**	30 minutes later	**G**	an hour later
B	the accident	**E**	Cologne	**H**	Bonn
C	yesterday evening	**F**	at home	**I**	the injured people

Example: There was an accident .... C ....

(i) The police arrived ....

(ii) Four people went to a hospital in ....

(iii) Two women are today ....

(iv) The police want information about ....

(Total for Question 30 = 4 marks)

A theft

A*   **31** Nele has had her purse stolen. Which statements are correct?

Listen and put a cross against the **four** correct answers.

Example: Nele was leaving the florist's.	X
(a) Nele saw the thief coming.	
(b) Nele could not see the thief coming.	
(c) Nele got a good look at the thief as he ran away.	
(d) Nele was too shocked to do anything.	
(e) The police were helpful.	
(f) The police were not interested.	
(g) She will find it hard to contact her friends now.	
(h) She is going to call all her friends now.	

(Total for Question 31 = 4 marks)

Money issues

 At a bank

E 32 You see this notice at the bank.

Ein neues Konto für Studenten

- Ab April gibt es ein tolles Konto für Sie!
- Sie brauchen nur €20 und Ihren Personalausweis.
- Sie können Ihre neue Bankkarte kostenlos in ganz Europa benutzen.
- Die ersten zwanzig Kunden bekommen auch ein kleines Geschenk!

Weitere Informationen finden Sie in der Broschüre.

Answer the questions in **English.** You don't need to write in sentences.

(a) When will the account be available?

.... **(1 mark)**

(b) What do you need to open an account? Give **one** example.

.... **(1 mark)**

(c) What will the first 20 customers receive?

.... **(1 mark)**

(d) Where will you find more information?

.... **(1 mark)**

(Total for Question 32 = 4 marks)

 Money problems

D 33 Robert has lost his job. What does he say? Listen and put a cross against the **four** correct answers.

Example: He lost his job last week.	X
(a) He has saved a lot of money for his holiday.	
(b) He thinks his mother may help him.	
(c) He has no birthday present for his girlfriend.	
(d) They are going to a restaurant.	
(e) He cannot pay at a restaurant.	
(f) He has no cash.	
(g) He still has money in his bank account.	
(h) His bank account is empty.	

Make sure you don't put more than **four** crosses.

(Total for Question 33 = 4 marks)

Problems at the station

Problems at the bus station

B 34 Read what these people have written in their blogs.

> **Max:**
> Heute früh hatte der Bus eine Panne und wir mussten am Busbahnhof warten, bis man ihn repariert hatte.

> **Fatima:**
> Gestern war der Fahrkartenautomat außer Betrieb und ich musste daher eine halbe Stunde am Schalter Schlange stehen.

> **Adam:**
> Der Busbahnhof ist immer sehr schmutzig und laut. Ich gehe nicht gern dahin.

> **Ben:**
> Letzte Woche wollte ich mit dem Bus nach Frankfurt fahren, aber ich fand die Fahrkarte wirklich teuer. Ich bin also mit dem Auto dahin gefahren.

> **Hanna:**
> Weil die alte Dame vor mir am Schalter alles so langsam machte, habe ich den Bus verpasst.

> **Kadir:**
> Die Busfahrerin war so unfreundlich und schlecht gelaunt, dass ich mich später beim Chef beschwert habe.

Who mentions what? Write the correct name in each box.

Example:	Unfriendly staff	Kadir
(a)	Machine not working	
(b)	Transport breakdown	
(c)	Price	
(d)	Cleanliness	

(Total for Question 34 = 4 marks)

Problems at the railway station

C 35 Verena has a problem at the station. Which statements are correct?
Listen and put a cross against the **four** correct answers.

Example: Verena is taking a train to Hamburg and then to Bremen.	X
(a) The train to Hamburg is fifteen minutes late.	
(b) The train to Hamburg is on time.	
(c) She will miss her connection to Bremen.	
(d) Verena will catch her connection to Bremen.	
(e) The next train to Bremen leaves at six in the morning.	
(f) The next train to Bremen leaves at five this evening.	
(g) Verena is not annoyed.	
(h) Verena is very angry.	

(Total for Question 35 = 4 marks)

Lost property

Lost property

C 36 You read Lena's email.

Löschen Antworten Antworten Alle Weiher Drucken

Ich glaube, ich habe heute Nachmittag meinen Schal im Kaufhaus verloren. Der Schal ist hellblau und aus Seide. Er war ein Geschenk von meiner Oma.

Ich war zuerst in der Herrenabteilung und dann bin ich mit dem Fahrstuhl zum dritten Stock gefahren, um ein Kleid zu suchen. Ich habe das Kleid anprobiert und vielleicht ist der Schal noch im Umkleideraum.

Ich wäre sehr dankbar, wenn Sie mir mailen oder mich anrufen könnten. Meine Telefonnummer ist 7 66 45 23.

Lena Schulz

What does Lena say? Put a cross in the **four** correct boxes.

Example:	Lena has lost something.	X
(a)	She lost it yesterday afternoon.	
(b)	She lost a silk scarf.	
(c)	Her grandma gave her the scarf.	
(d)	She took the lift to the 2nd floor.	
(e)	She tried on a dress.	
(f)	She dropped the item on the escalator.	
(g)	She is going to phone the department store.	
(h)	She wants someone to contact her.	

(Total for Question 36 = 4 marks)

What have they lost?

G 37 What items have these people lost? Listen and put a cross in the correct box.

	A	B	C	D	E	F
Example:				X		
(i)						
(ii)						
(iii)						
(iv)						

(Total for Question 37 = 4 marks)

Complaints

A problem in a department store

38 You read this report about a problem in a store.

> Heute früh waren Hunderte Leute im Kaufhaus, um verschiedene reduzierte Sachen wie Kleidung oder Elektrogeräte im Sommerschlussverkauf zu kaufen.
>
> Man konnte sich kaum bewegen und es gab viel Lärm. Plötzlich hat man einen lauten Schrei gehört und eine alte Frau war am Boden. Das Bein hat ihr weh getan und sie hat geweint. Ein Mädchen hatte versucht, ihr Portemonnaie zu stehlen, als die Frau es aus der Handtasche genommen hat.
>
> Aber das Mädchen ist ohne das Portemonnaie weggelaufen und ein junger Verkäufer ist ihr gefolgt. Die Kunden neben der Kasse waren sehr freundlich und haben der Frau geholfen. Der Verkäufer hat das Mädchen neben der Rolltreppe festgehalten.
>
> Jemand hat die Polizei angerufen, und das Mädchen musste zur Polizeiwache gehen. Weil die Frau einen Schock hatte, hat der Geschäftsleiter sie in ein Nebenzimmer gebracht. Dort konnte sie sich ein bisschen ausruhen, bevor sie nach Hause gegangen ist. Sie war so dankbar, dass sie dem Verkäufer Geld geben wollte.

A   What happened? Put a cross in the correct box.

(a) Das Kaufhaus war...

(i)	leer.	
(ii)	ruhig.	
(iii)	überfüllt.	

(c) Der Verkäufer ist…

(i)	dem Mädchen nachgelaufen.	
(ii)	zur Polizei gegangen.	
(iii)	zu Boden gefallen.	

(b) Das Mädchen hat…

(i)	ein Portemonnaie gestohlen.	
(ii)	nichts gestohlen.	
(iii)	eine Handtasche gestohlen.	

(d) Die Frau ist…

(i)	gleich nach Hause gegangen.	
(ii)	länger im Kaufhaus geblieben.	
(iii)	zur Polizeiwache gegangen.	

B   Put a cross next to the **four** correct statements.

Example:	Es gab Sonderangebote im Kaufhaus.	X
(a)	Die Kunden wollten billig einkaufen.	
(b)	Sie wollten nur Kleidung kaufen.	
(c)	Die Frau war jung.	
(d)	Sie ist gefallen.	
(e)	Sie hatte Kopfschmerzen.	
(f)	Das Mädchen wollte der Frau helfen.	
(g)	Die anderen Kunden waren nett.	
(h)	Die Frau wollte dem Verkäufer danken.	

(Total for Question 38 = 8 marks)

School subjects

 School subjects

F 1 Read what these teenagers say about school subjects.

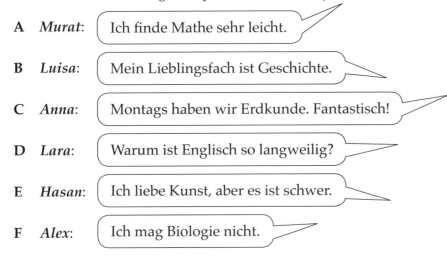

A *Murat*: Ich finde Mathe sehr leicht.

B *Luisa*: Mein Lieblingsfach ist Geschichte.

C *Anna*: Montags haben wir Erdkunde. Fantastisch!

D *Lara*: Warum ist Englisch so langweilig?

E *Hasan*: Ich liebe Kunst, aber es ist schwer.

F *Alex*: Ich mag Biologie nicht.

Which subjects do they mention? Write the correct letter in the box.

Example:	Art	E
(i)	Maths	
(ii)	Geography	
(iii)	Biology	
(iv)	History	

(Total for Question 1 = 4 marks)

 School

G 2 Which subjects do these students enjoy? Listen and put a cross in the correct box.

	A Physics	B Geography	C Art	D German	E DT	F History
Example: Bierta					X	
(i) Ilayda						
(ii) Celina						
(iii) Romeo						
(iv) Eva						

(Total for Question 2 = 4 marks)

> • Think of the German words for the subject before you listen.
> • Be careful to put the cross under the correct subject.

Opinions about school

My school

C

3   Read what Esma says about her school.

> Ich finde meine Gesamtschule toll.
>
> Ich glaube, dass viele Schulregeln fair sind. Rauchen ist verboten und das ist gut. Aber ich finde es doof, dass Kaugummi in den Klassenzimmern verboten ist.
>
> Die Lehrer sind oft nett, aber die Kunstlehrerin ist sehr streng und unfreundlich. Mein Lieblingsfach ist Geschichte und der Lehrer ist sehr lustig. Mathe finde ich sehr schwer und ich habe immer Angst, wenn wir eine Klassenarbeit haben.
>
> Nach der Schule gibt es viele AGs. Mittwochs mache ich Tanzen und freitags spiele ich im Schulorchester. Ich mache nie Turnen, weil es langweilig ist.

> If you are not sure which answer is correct, try to decide which ones are definitely wrong.

Put a cross in the correct box.

(a) Esma thinks the rule about chewing gum is…

(i)	stupid.	
(ii)	fair.	
(iii)	good.	

(b) The Art teacher is…

(i)	friendly.	
(ii)	strict.	
(iii)	funny.	

(c) She is scared of tests in…

(i)	Maths.	
(ii)	History.	
(iii)	Art.	

(d) On Wednesdays after school she…

(i)	does gymnastics.	
(ii)	does dance.	
(iii)	plays in the orchestra.	

(Total for Question 3 = 4 marks)

Exchange visit

A*

4   You hear a conversation about a school exchange visit to England. Listen and put a cross against the **four** correct answers.

Example: There was a school exchange to England.	X
(a) The majority of pupils enjoyed the visit.	
(b) The German and English pupils did not get on.	
(c) Many of the pupils were homesick.	
(d) The exchange visit went smoothly.	
(e) On the previous exchange a pupil was injured.	
(f) On the previous exchange nobody wanted to come home early.	
(g) The German pupils were amazed by the English school rules.	
(h) The German pupils found the English rules similar to their own.	

(Total for Question 4 = 4 marks)

School routine

School routine

C   **5**   Read Tom's email about his school day.

> Löschen   Antworten   Antworten Alle   Weiher   Drueken
>
> Ich muss während der Woche sehr früh aufstehen. Nach dem Frühstück gehe ich zu Fuß zur Schule und plaudere mit meinen Freunden auf dem Schulhof.
>
> Die Schule beginnt um acht Uhr und wir haben um halb zehn eine kleine Pause. Dienstag ist mein Lieblingstag, weil wir eine Doppelstunde Erdkunde haben. Die Lehrerin ist toll und sehr lustig.
>
> Ich esse jeden Tag in der Kantine zu Mittag. Nach der Schule gibt es viele AGs und ich treibe sehr gern Sport. Abends mache ich viele Hausaufgaben. Leider!

What does Tom mention? Put a cross in the **four** correct boxes.

Example:	Tom gets up early.	X
(a)	He walks to school.	
(b)	He chats to friends on the way.	
(c)	School starts at 08.00.	
(d)	The morning break is at 10.30.	
(e)	He loves Tuesdays.	
(f)	The Geography teacher is strict.	
(g)	He has lunch in the canteen.	
(h)	He doesn't get much homework.	

(Total for Question 5 = 4 marks)

Around school

D   **6**   Where are these pupils going?

A canteen	**D** classroom
B hall	**E** library
C playground	**F** staffroom

Listen and put a cross in the correct box.

	A	**B**	**C**	**D**	**E**	**F**
Example:				X		
(i)						
(ii)						
(iii)						
(iv)						

(Total for Question 6 = 4 marks)

German schools

German schools

B 7 What does Max write about schools?

> Ich besuche ein Gymnasium mit etwa tausend Schülern und Schülerinnen. Die Realschule in der Nähe ist noch größer. Ich finde meine Schule toll. Die Lehrer sind fantastisch und viele Schüler bekommen bei den Prüfungen sehr gute Noten.
>
> Ich war auch in der Grundschule sehr glücklich. Sie war ziemlich klein und ich hatte viele Freunde.
>
> Der erste Tag am Gymnasium war furchtbar. Das Schulgebäude war so groß, und ich konnte das richtige Klassenzimmer nicht finden.
>
> Jetzt bin ich in der zehnten Klasse und ich finde die Schule ziemlich schwer. Ich brauche sehr gute Noten, weil ich in die Oberstufe gehen will. Ich will nicht sitzen bleiben!

Put a cross in the **four** correct boxes.

Example:	Max goes to a grammar school.	X
(a)	The secondary school has 1,000 students.	
(b)	Many students at his school do well in exams.	
(c)	He liked primary school.	
(d)	His first day at grammar school was great.	
(e)	He had problems finding classrooms at first.	
(f)	He finds school easy now.	
(g)	He wants to go into the sixth form.	
(h)	He has to repeat a year.	

> Read each statement **very** carefully.

(Total for Question 7 = 4 marks)

An English school

A 8 Aylin is describing her new school. Listen and answer the questions in English.

(a) What did Aylin particularly like about her school in Switzerland? Give **two** details.

  (i) ....

  .... **(1 mark)**

  (ii) ....

  .... **(1 mark)**

(b) What does she think about her new school?

  (i) Positive: ....

  .... **(1 mark)**

  (ii) Negative: ....

  .... **(1 mark)**

(Total for Question 8 = 4 marks)

Primary school

At primary school

C

9 You read these comments.

Mina:	Die Grundschule hat viel Spaß gemacht und ich hatte viele Freunde.
Ben:	Die Grundschullehrer waren sehr freundlich und lustig. Sie waren nie schlecht gelaunt.
Tom:	Es war besser, weil wir keine Hausaufgaben hatten. Nach der Schule konnten wir spielen.
Lena:	Ich musste jeden Tag mit der Straßenbahn zur Schule fahren, aber es war nicht zu weit.
Susi:	Die Grundschule war toll, weil der Schultag nicht so lang war. Wir hatten den ganzen Nachmittag frei.
Eric:	Ich habe in der Grundschule Englisch gelernt. Es war furchtbar, weil der Lehrer so langweilig war.

Who says what? Write the correct name in the box.

Who…

Example:	found primary school fun?	Mina
(a)	had nice teachers?	
(b)	didn't like learning a foreign language?	
(c)	went to school by public transport?	
(d)	liked the shorter school day?	

(Total for Question 9 = 4 marks)

The difference between primary and secondary school

B

10 Petra and Hannes are talking about school.

What did they used to do at primary school and what do they do at secondary school?

Listen and write in the correct letter.

A eat fruit	**C** play	**E** draw
B sing	**D** study	**F** swim

Primary school	Secondary school
Example: B	
(i)	**(iii)**
(ii)	**(iv)**

(Total for Question 10 = 4 marks)

Issues at school

Notices in school

F **11** You see these notices in school.

A
> **Morgen schlechtes Wetter. Schulfrei.**

D
> **Lehrerzimmer. Bitte warten.**

F
> Die Kantine ist heute geschlossen.

B
> Heute sind keine AGs.

E
> **Du darfst in der Schule nicht rauchen.**

C
> **Bitte nicht eintreten.** 🚫

What do these signs mean? Write the correct letter in the box.

> Read each notice carefully and look for key words.

Example:	Please wait!	D
(i)	No smoking	
(ii)	A day off tomorrow	
(iii)	Canteen closed	
(iv)	No clubs	

(Total for Question 11 = 4 marks)

School issues

G **12** What do these people say about their school? Listen and put a cross in the correct box.

Example: There are lots of…

(i)	teachers.	
(ii)	clubs.	X
(iii)	lessons.	

(a) On Thursday there is…

(i)	volleyball.	
(ii)	chess club.	
(iii)	orchestra.	

(b) There are friendly…

(i)	secretaries.	
(ii)	teachers.	
(iii)	sixth formers.	

(c) You are not allowed to have…

(i)	chewing gum.	
(ii)	a mobile phone.	
(iii)	trainers.	

(d) This pupil has to wear…

(i)	a uniform.	
(ii)	a coat.	
(iii)	black shoes.	

(Total for Question 12 = 4 marks)

Future education plans

Future education plans

13 You read this email from Melisa.

Hallo Laura,

gestern habe ich die letzte Prüfung für die Mittlere Reife geschrieben und ich bin sehr nervös! Ich brauche gute Noten, um in die beste Oberstufenschule in der Gegend zu gehen.

Bevor das nächste Trimester anfängt, will ich mich mit Freunden in Spanien erholen und chillen, weil ich ab September besonders fleißig arbeiten muss.

Als ich jünger war, wollte ich Krankenschwester werden. Aber letztes Jahr fand ich das Arbeitspraktikum bei einem Tierarzt so fantastisch, dass ich jetzt mit Tieren arbeiten will.

Nach der Oberstufe möchte ich an der Uni einen guten Kurs für Tierärzte machen. Als Student ist es zwar billiger, zu Hause zu wohnen, aber ich will lieber in eine andere Stadt umziehen. Nach dem Studium will ich mit Tieren in Afrika arbeiten.

Also, schöne Ferien! Tschüs.

Melisa

Answer the questions in **English**.

(a) What did Melisa do yesterday?

.... **(1 mark)**

(b) Which sixth form does she want to go to?

.... **(1 mark)**

(c) What does she want to do before next term?

.... **(1 mark)**

(d) Why does she need to do that?

.... **(1 mark)**

(e) How did work experience influence her?

.... **(1 mark)**

(f) What does she want to do at university?

.... **(1 mark)**

(g) Where would she prefer to live as a student?

.... **(1 mark)**

(h) What does she want to do when she qualifies?

.... **(1 mark)**

(**Total for Question 13 = 8 marks**)

Future careers

Future plans

A*

14 You read this article.

> Die Oberstufe und die Uni sind bei Jugendlichen nicht immer beliebt. Einige machen lieber eine Lehre. Mina (16) will eine Lehre als Friseuse machen und gleich ein bisschen Geld verdienen. Sie meint: „Wenn ich später zu Hause Kinder habe, möchte ich halbtags in einem Friseursalon arbeiten."
>
> Einige junge Leute studieren an der Uni, um in Zukunft einen guten Beruf und ein hoher Gehalt zu haben. Sie hoffen dann, einen tollen Lebensstil zu haben. Mustafa (18) will viel verdienen und in verschiedenen Ländern wie Indien oder Russland Urlaub machen.
>
> Wenn man immer im Freien sein will, dann ist zum Beispiel Büroarbeit nicht ideal. Laras Arbeitspraktikum in einem Büro war furchtbar. Sie will jetzt Gärtnerin werden. Sie sagt: „Auch im Winter oder bei schlechtem Wetter arbeite ich lieber im Freien."
>
> Manchmal arbeiten junge Leute als Freiwillige im Ausland. Nach dem Abitur plant Ben (15), ein Jahr freiwillig in Afrika zu arbeiten. Er sagt: „Ich möchte in einer Grundschule aushelfen und auch viel über das Leben in Afrika lernen."

A   Put a cross in the correct box.

Example: Jugendliche wie Mina wollen…

(i)	eine Lehre machen.	X
(ii)	in die Oberstufe gehen.	
(iii)	einen Studienplatz finden.	

(a) Wenn sie Mutter wird, will Mina…

(i)	Teilzeit arbeiten.	
(ii)	nur zu Hause arbeiten.	
(iii)	jeden Tag zu Hause bleiben.	

(b) Mustafa möchte…

(i)	nur in Deutschland reisen.	
(ii)	ins Ausland reisen.	
(iii)	nur in Indien reisen.	

(c) Laras Arbeitspraktikum war…

(i)	eine tolle Überraschung.	
(ii)	eine gute Erfahrung.	
(iii)	ein enttäuschendes Erlebnis.	

(d) Ben wird in Afrika…

(i)	nichts verdienen.	
(ii)	wenig verdienen.	
(iii)	gut verdienen.	

B   Put a cross next to the **four** correct statements.

Example:	Mina will einen Beruf haben.	X
(a)	Mina wird sofort ein Gehalt bekommen.	
(b)	Mina will mit Kindern arbeiten.	
(c)	Mustafa möchte eine gut bezahlte Stelle.	
(d)	Mustafa will in anderen Ländern wohnen.	
(e)	Lara will in einem Büro arbeiten.	
(f)	Lara arbeitet gern das ganze Jahr im Garten.	
(g)	Ben wird in die Oberstufe gehen.	
(h)	Ben findet nur europäische Länder interessant.	

(Total for Question 14 = 8 marks)

Jobs

 Jobs

G 15 Read these jobs.

| Metzger | Lehrer | Bäcker | Elektriker | Arzt |

Which jobs are they? Put a cross in the **four** correct boxes.

Example:	Teacher	X
(a)	Police officer	
(b)	Doctor	
(c)	Engineer	
(d)	Mechanic	
(e)	Baker	
(f)	Dentist	
(g)	Butcher	
(h)	Electrician	

(Total for Question 15 = 4 marks)

 What do these people do?

D 16 What are these people's jobs? Listen and put a cross in the correct box.

A teacher	C nurse	E butcher
B vet	D lorry driver	F police officer

	A	B	C	D	E	F
Example: Silas						X
(i) Philipp						
(ii) Özlem						
(iii) Christoph						
(iv) Gerhard						

(Total for Question 16 = 4 marks)

Before you listen, think of the German words for these jobs so that you are well prepared.

75

Job adverts

A job advertisement

E   **17** You read this advertisement.

——— KELLNER GESUCHT ———

Sind Sie fleißig und freundlich? Wollen Sie in einem modernen Restaurant arbeiten?

Wir suchen einen Kellner für das italienische Restaurant am Dom.

Arbeitsstunden: Freitags und samstags 18:00–23:00 Uhr, sonntags 12:00–16:00 Uhr.

Sie bekommen €8,50 pro Stunde.

Tel.: 8 76 35 44

Answer the questions in **English.**

(a) What sort of person is needed? Give **one** example. .... **(1 mark)**

(b) What is the job? .... **(1 mark)**

(c) When do you start on Sunday? .... **(1 mark)**

(d) What is the hourly pay? .... **(1 mark)**

(Total for Question 17 = 4 marks)

A job advert

B   **18** Lars is talking about a job advert he has seen. Listen and complete the sentences by entering the correct letter at the end of each sentence.

A boring	**D** his mother's office	**G** good
B half past four	**E** the cinema	**H** half past five
C the youth club	**F** the travel agency	**I** the sports centre

Write the **four** correct letters in the boxes below.

Example: The job is in ☐ F .

(i) Lars has worked in ☐ .

(ii) Lars thinks office work is ☐ .

(iii) He is pleased the job finishes at ☐ .

(iv) On Saturday evenings Lars likes to go to ☐ or ☐ .

(Total for Question 18 = 4 marks)

CV

Leni's CV

D

19 You read Leni's CV.

Complete the details about Leni's CV. Write the correct letter to complete each sentence.

A	electrician
B	tennis
C	waitress
D	Frankfurt
E	dancing
F	comprehensive school
G	shop assistant
H	mechanic
I	grammar school

Name: Leni Weigel   D

Example: She was born in ....

(i) She goes to a ....

(ii) She works as a ....

(iii) Her favourite hobby is ....

(iv) She wants to become a ....

LEBENSLAUF

Name: Leni Weigel

Geburtsdatum:
Ich bin am 2. April 1995 in Frankfurt geboren.

Schule:
Ich gehe auf eine Gesamtschule und bekomme gute Noten und Zeugnisse. Mein Lieblingsfach ist Englisch und ich mag auch Geschichte.

Arbeitserfahrung:
Samstags und sonntags arbeite ich als Kellnerin in einem Café und ich finde die Arbeit interessant.

Interessen:
Ich habe viele Hobbys, aber am liebsten tanze ich. Ich gehe zweimal pro Woche in eine Tanzschule. Ich spiele am Wochenende Tennis.

Zukunftspläne:
In der Zukunft möchte ich Mechanikerin werden.

(Total for Question 19 = 4 marks)

Martha's CV

E

20 Martha is talking about her CV. Listen and complete the details in the form in **English**.

Example: Surname: ......Wolf...

(a) Age: ....

(b) School: ....

(c) Work experience location: ....

(d) Characteristics: hard-working and ....

(Total for Question 20 = 4 marks)

Job application

A job application

C **21** Hannah is applying for a job.

Do the activities belong in the past, present or future?

Put a cross in the **four** correct boxes.

> Look for key verbs (arbeiten, lernen) and signs of tenses (Letzten August, später).

Sehr geehrte Frau Braun,

ich möchte in den Sommerferien im Verkehrsamt arbeiten und kann am 7. Juli anfangen. Ich möchte vier Wochen arbeiten.

Ich habe ein Jahr in London gewohnt und spreche gut Englisch. Ich lerne in der Schule auch Spanisch.

Letzten August habe ich drei Wochen in einem Reisebüro gearbeitet und fand das sehr interessant.

Später möchte ich Fremdsprachen studieren und dann in Spanien oder England arbeiten.

Mit freundlichen Grüßen

Ihre

Hannah Schulz

		Past	Present	Future
Example:	Working in a tourist office			X
(a)	Living in London			
(b)	Learning Spanish			
(c)	Working in a travel agency			
(d)	Working in Spain			

(Total for Question 21 = 4 marks)

Job application

F **22** What details do these people give about their job application?

A references	**C** office work experience	**E** enclosing CV
B 11 o'clock interview	**D** start on 1st July	**F** speaks a foreign language

Listen and put a cross in the correct box.

	A	**B**	**C**	**D**	**E**	**F**
Example:					X	
(i)						
(ii)						
(iii)						
(iv)						

(Total for Question 22 = 4 marks)

Job interview

Job interview

23 Listen to this telephone interview. Choose the correct ending for each sentence.

Example: The job interview is for the position of…

(i)	waiter.	X
(ii)	tutor.	
(iii)	shop assistant.	

(a) Sebastian has…

(i)	no relevant work experience.	
(ii)	never worked at a guest house.	
(iii)	relevant work experience.	

(b) At the end of the summer Sebastian…

(i)	gave in his notice.	
(ii)	would have liked to stay longer.	
(iii)	was really bored.	

(c) The guests were surprised by…

(i)	how impatient Sebastian was.	
(ii)	how helpful Sebastian was.	
(iii)	how patient Sebastian's colleague was.	

(d) Sebastian wants the job…

(i)	because it is his dream job.	
(ii)	because it involves travel.	
(iii)	because it will look good on his CV.	

(Total for Question 23 = 4 marks)

Opinions about jobs

Opinions about jobs

B

24 Read these people's views.

Susi:	Ich glaube, es ist nicht notwendig, einen hohen Lohn zu bekommen.
Luis:	Wenn man ganztags arbeitet, bekommt man mehr Geld.
Lina:	Ich finde meinen Job sehr schwer, weil ich von 23:00 bis 06:00 Uhr arbeiten muss.
Elif:	Es ist eine sehr gute Erfahrung, wenn man als Schüler einen Nebenjob hat.
Mia:	Der Vorteil ist, dass die Arbeit nicht zu schwer ist. Dann bin ich abends nicht so müde.
Jan:	Ich denke, es ist für mich nicht so gut, ganztags zu arbeiten, weil ich mehr Freizeit haben will.
Ozan:	Ich komme mit den anderen Arbeitern in der Fabrik sehr gut aus. Das ist sehr wichtig für mich.

Which people suggest the following? Write the correct name in the box.

It is…

Example:	good to have work experience.	Elif
(a)	important to get on well with colleagues.	
(b)	not necessary to earn a lot.	
(c)	better to work part-time.	
(d)	hard working nights.	

(Total for Question 24 = 4 marks)

A new job

A

25 Ben is talking about his new job. Listen and answer the questions in English.

(a) What was Ben's task on his first day at work?

.... **(1 mark)**

(b) What did the boss often do in front of the customers?

.... **(1 mark)**

(c) Why would Ben recommend working at the department store? Give **two** reasons.

.... **(1 mark)**

.... **(1 mark)**

(Total for Question 25 = 4 marks)

> Make sure you read the questions carefully and answer concisely as possible. You don't have to answer in full sentences.

Part-time work

Part-time jobs

26 You see this article about part-time jobs.

> **Mina (14)** trägt jeden Tag Zeitungen aus. Sie findet es schwer, weil sie so früh aufstehen muss, aber sie braucht das Geld für den Sommerurlaub.
>
> **Felix (18)** arbeitet samstags in einem Supermarkt. Es macht ihm viel Spaß, obwohl er abends sehr müde ist. Das Beste ist, wenn er an der Kasse arbeiten kann, weil er sehr gern mit den Kunden spricht.
>
> **Mehmet (17)** hilft seinem Onkel, der ein türkisches Restaurant hat. Am Anfang musste er das Geschirr abwaschen, aber jetzt darf er als Kellner arbeiten und das findet er viel interessanter.
>
> **Hannah (16)** arbeitet am Wochenende mit ihrer Mutter, die Gärtnerin ist. Hannah macht das freiwillig, weil sie gern im Freien ist. Außerdem will auch sie später einmal Gärtnerin werden.

Answer the questions in **English.**

> Keep your answers simple and clear.

(a) What is Mina's job?

.... **(1 mark)**

(b) What doesn't she like about it?

.... **(1 mark)**

(c) What is the disadvantage of Felix's job?

.... **(1 mark)**

(d) Which task does he most enjoy?

.... **(1 mark)**

(e) Where does Mehmet work?

.... **(1 mark)**

(f) Why is the job more interesting now?

.... **(1 mark)**

(g) What does Hannah like about her job?

.... **(1 mark)**

(h) Why is the work good experience for her?

.... **(1 mark)**

(Total for Question 26 = 8 marks)

My work experience

Emine's work experience

E   27 Read Emine's blog about her work experience.

Ich mache mein Betriebspraktikum in einem Geschäft.

Jeden Tag fahre ich mit der Straßenbahn zur Arbeit. Ich arbeite acht Stunden pro Tag und am Abend bin ich sehr müde.

Der Chef ist sehr nett und ich finde die Arbeit toll. Ich helfe im Geschäft und koche Kaffee.

> Write in **English.**
> Answers in German will gain no marks.

Answer the questions in **English.**

(a) Where is Emine working?   .... **(1 mark)**

(b) How many hours does she work per day?   .... **(1 mark)**

(c) What is the manager like?   .... **(1 mark)**

(d) What does she think of the work?   .... **(1 mark)**

(Total for Question 27 = 4 marks)

Sol's work experience

C   28 Sol is talking about his work experience. What does he mention?

Listen and put a cross in the **four** correct boxes.

Example: Where he worked.	X
(a) The other employees.	
(b) His journey to work.	
(c) What he did at lunchtime.	
(d) Disadvantages of this kind of work.	
(e) What he had to wear.	
(f) What he had to do.	
(g) The days he worked.	
(h) The work he wants to do in the future.	

(Total for Question 28 = 4 marks)

> Read the options carefully before you listen to get an idea of what the text may be about.

Work experience

Work experience

29 You read this article.

Letzten Monat hat Lukas (16) ein Arbeitspraktikum in einer Autofabrik gemacht. Er sagt: „Es war eine tolle Erfahrung, weil ich Autos liebe." Am ersten Tag hat er Akten sortiert und Telefonanrufe beantwortet. Er sagt: „Ich habe mich ein bisschen gelangweilt, aber es hat mir gefallen, Kontakt mit Kunden zu haben."

Die nächsten acht Tage war die Arbeit viel interessanter, weil er in der Werkstatt arbeiten durfte. Lukas: „Es war fantastisch! Hunderte Autos auf einem langen Fließband!" Weil die anderen Kollegen sehr freundlich und geduldig waren, hat er viel gelernt.

Lukas glaubt, dass es am besten war, als er einmal mit dem Chef zur Messe gefahren ist. Er sagt: „Ich fand es höchst interessant, mit den Vertretern zu sprechen. Sie waren sehr hilfsbereit und der Chef hat mir auch viele Ratschläge gegeben."

Der Chef, Herr Lehmann, sagt: „Lukas war ein sehr begeisterter Schüler. In der Zukunft würde ich ihm gerne eine Stelle anbieten."

> Base all your answers on the text, not on your general experience.

(a) Choose the correct ending for each statement.

(i) Das Arbeitspraktikum…	**A** hat er mit Wagen gearbeitet.
(ii) Am ersten Tag…	**B** hat er eine Stelle gefunden.
(iii) Ab dem zweiten Tag…	**C** war ein sehr gutes Erlebnis.
(iv) Auf der Messe…	**D** hat er sich mit anderen unterhalten.
(v) Während des Arbeitspraktikums…	**E** hat Lukas einen guten Eindruck gemacht.
	F musste er Büroarbeit machen.

Example: (i) ......C......

(ii) ....   **(iii)** ....   **(iv)** ....   **(v)** ....

(b) Put a cross by the **four** correct statements.

Example:	Lukas fand das Praktikum gut.	X
(i)	Zuerst war die Arbeit nicht sehr interessant.	
(ii)	Er fand die Kunden nervig.	
(iii)	Die Werkstattarbeit hat ihm wenig Spaß gemacht.	
(iv)	Er fand die Mitarbeiter nett.	
(v)	Er ist mit dem Geschäftsleiter in eine Fabrik gegangen.	
(vi)	Der Chef wollte ihm helfen.	
(vii)	Lukas hat nicht fleißig gearbeitet.	
(viii)	Herr Lehmann möchte Lukas einen Job geben.	

(Total for Question 29 = 8 marks)

Dialogues and messages

Mobile phones

F **30** Where do they use their phones?

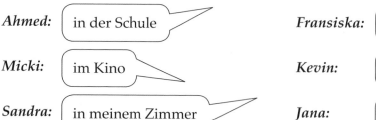

Ahmed: in der Schule   *Fransiska:* im Einfaufzentrum

Micki: im Kino   *Kevin:* im Zug

Sandra: in meinem Zimmer   *Jana:* in der Stadt

Put a cross in the four correct boxes.

	Micki	Ahmed	Sandra	Fransiska	Kevin	Jana
Example: at school						
(i) at home						
(ii) on the train						
(iii) at the shopping centre						
(iv) in town						

(Total for Question 30 = 4 marks)

Leaving a message

E **31** Max is ringing Ina's home number. Listen and put a cross in the correct box.

Example:

Max wants to speak to…

(i)	Ina.	X
(ii)	Ina's dad.	
(iii)	Ina's mum.	

(a) Ina has gone into town…

(i)	by bus.	
(ii)	by bike.	
(iii)	on foot.	

(b) Ina has gone into town to…

(i)	see a film.	
(ii)	go for a meal.	
(iii)	go shopping.	

(c) This evening Ina has got to…

(i)	do homework.	
(ii)	practise the piano.	
(iii)	have her evening meal.	

(d) Max will see Ina tomorrow…

(i)	at the youth club.	
(ii)	at the cinema.	
(iii)	at school.	

(Total for Question 31 = 4 marks)

Language of the internet

Information technology

G **32** Look at these words used in ICT.

A	Bildschirm	D	Tastatur	D	Kennwort

B	Maus	E	Computer	E	Webseite

Write the correct letter in the box.

Example:	Web page	F
(i)	Keyboard	
(ii)	Screen	
(iii)	Password	
(iv)	Mouse	

(Total for Question 32 = 4 marks)

IT problems

F **33** What do these people have a problem with?

A	printer out of paper	D	computer not working

B	email not working	E	no internet connection

C	dirty screen	F	missing mouse

> Revise computer and internet language before you try this question. Then read options A–F and think of the vocabulary you might hear.

Put a cross in the correct box.

	A	**B**	**C**	**D**	**E**	**F**
Example:					X	
(i)						
(ii)						
(iii)						
(iv)						

(Total for Question 33 = 4 marks)

Internet pros and cons

Pros and cons of the internet

D   **34** Read what these teenagers think about the internet.

Max: Ich vergesse immer mein Kennwort. Das ist dumm!

Tom: Ich kann meinem Freund in den USA E-Mails schreiben.

Adam: Ich finde es sehr nützlich für die Schularbeiten.

Lara: Ich glaube, das Internet kann manchmal gefährlich sein.

Lilli: Es gibt viele tolle Webseiten. Ich kann alles online finden.

Mina: Ich chatte online zu viel mit Freunden und meine Eltern finden das ärgerlich!

Who says what? Write the correct name in each box.

Example:	I chat too much online.	Mina
(a)	I think the internet can be dangerous.	
(b)	I find it useful for school work.	
(c)	I can email my friend.	
(d)	I can find everything online.	

(Total for Question 34 = 4 marks)

Internet

C   **35** What do Markus and Sandra think about the internet? Listen and put a cross in the correct box.

	Markus	**Sandra**
Example: frustrating	X	
(a) too expensive		
(b) useful for homework		
(c) forgets password		
(d) good for communicating		

(Total for Question 35 = 4 marks)

Gender and plurals

In the nominative, German nouns are either *der* (masculine), *die* (feminine) or *das* (neuter).
der / *die* / *das* = the

  der Hund   **die** Katze   **das** Pferd

A Put a circle round the correct article.

1 der / die / das Mülleimer (*m.*)   6 der / die / das Restaurant (*n.*)

2 der / die / das Kino (*n.*)   7 der / die / das Autobahn (*f.*)

3 der / die / das Krankenschwester (*f.*)   8 der / die / das Sportlehrer (*m.*)

4 der / die / das Rucksack (*m.*)   9 der / die / das Umwelt (*f.*)

5 der / die / das Handy (*n.*)

B Complete with *der*, *die* or *das*.

1 .... Haus ist modern. (*n.*)   5 .... Zug fährt langsam. (*m.*)

2 .... Schüler heißt Max. (*m.*)   6 .... Sparkasse ist geschlossen. (*f.*)

3 .... Schülerin heißt Demet. (*f.*)   7 .... Zeitung kostet 1 Euro. (*f.*)

4 .... Computer ist kaputt. (*m.*)   8 .... Buch ist langweilig. (*n.*)

In the accusative, the article *der* changes to *den* (masculine), but *die* and *das* don't change.

	m.	*f.*	*n.*	*pl.*
Accusative	**den**	die	das	die

  Wir mögen **den** Sportlehrer.

C Write in *den*, *die* or *das*.

1 Wir haben .... Pizza gegessen. (*f.*)   4 Vati kauft .... Pullover. (*m.*)

2 Wir können .... Krankenhaus   5 Liest du .... Buch? (*n.*)
  sehen. (*n.*)   6 Ich mähe .... Rasen. (*m.*)

3 Ich mache .... Hausaufgabe. (*f.*)

German plurals come in many forms. The most common ones are *–e* and *–n*, but many are irregular, maybe adding an umlaut or simply staying the same.

(S) Brief   ⟶   (P) Brief**e**
(S) Tasse   ⟶   (P) Tasse**n**
(S) Teller ⟶   (P) Teller
(S) Glas   ⟶   (P) Gl**ä**s**er**

D Write **S** if the noun is singular and **P** if it is plural. If it could be either, put **E**.

Haus ...., Buch ...., Männer ...., Autos ...., Häuser ...., Supermarkt ....,

Tisch ...., Mann ...., Supermärkte ...., Tische ...., Handys ....,

Zimmer ...., Bilder ...., Computer ....

Cases 1

> The prepositions which trigger a change to the accusative are *für, um, durch, gegen, bis* and *ohne*.
>
> | | *m.* | *f.* | *n.* | *pl.* |
> |---|---|---|---|---|
> | **Nominative** | der | die | das | die |
> | **Accusative** | den | die | das | die |
> | | | | | |
> | **Nominative** | ein | eine | ein | keine |
> | **Accusative** | einen | eine | ein | keine |

A Write in *den, die, das, einen, eine* or *ein*.

1 um .... Ecke (*round the corner*) (*f.*)

2 durch .... Stadt (*through the town*) (*f.*)

3 ohne .... Auto (*without a car*) (*n.*)

4 für .... Schule (*for the school*) (*f.*)

5 für .... Freund (*for a friend*) (*m.*)

6 gegen .... Wand (*against the wall*) (*f.*)

7 durch .... Wald (*through a wood*) (*m.*)

> The prepositions which trigger a change to the dative are: *aus, außer, bei, gegenüber, mit, nach, seit, von* and *zu*.
>
> | | *m.* | *f.* | *n.* | *pl.* |
> |---|---|---|---|---|
> | **Nominative** | der | die | das | die |
> | **Dative** | dem | der | dem | den |
> | | | | | |
> | **Nominative** | ein | eine | ein | keine |
> | **Dative** | einem | einer | einem | keinen |

B Write in *dem, der, einem* or *einer*.

1 mit .... Bus (*by bus*) (*m.*)

2 seit .... Sommer (*since the summer*) (*m.*)

3 zu .... Bank (*to the bank*) (*f.*)

4 nach .... Party (*after the party*) (*f.*)

5 bei .... Freund (*at a friend's house*) (*m.*)

6 von .... Onkel (*from an uncle*) (*m.*)

7 gegenüber .... Tankstelle (*opposite the petrol station*) (*f.*)

8 außer .... Lehrerin (*apart from the teacher*) (*f.*)

> A few prepositions trigger a change to the genitive: *während, trotz* and *wegen*.
>
> | | *m.* | *f.* | *n.* | *pl.* |
> |---|---|---|---|---|
> | **Nominative** | der | die | das | die |
> | **Genitive** | des | der | des | der |
> | | | | | |
> | **Nominative** | ein | eine | ein | keine |
> | **Genitive** | eines | einer | eines | keinen |

C Write in *der* or *des*.

1 wegen .... Wetters (*because of the weather*) (*n.*)

2 während .... Stunde (*during the lesson*) (*f.*)

3 trotz .... Regens (*despite the rain*) (*m.*)

Cases 2

These prepositions trigger a change to the accusative if there is movement towards a place, or the dative if there is no movement:

an (on, at)	*auf* (on)	*hinter* (behind)
in (in)	*neben* (next to)	*über* (over, above)
unter (under)	*vor* (in front of)	*zwischen* (between)

See page 88 for the accusative and dative forms of articles.

A Circle the correct article.

1 Wir fahren in **der** / **die** Stadt. (*f.*)

2 Meine Schwester ist in **der** / **die** Schule. (*f.*)

3 Das Essen liegt auf **den** / **dem** Tisch. (*m.*)

4 Ich steige auf **die** / **der** Mauer. (*f.*)

5 Wir hängen das Bild an **der** / **die** Wand. (*f.*)

6 Jetzt ist das Bild an **der** / **die** Wand. (*f.*)

7 Die Katze läuft hinter **einen** / **einem** Schrank. (*m.*)

8 Wo ist die Katze jetzt? Hinter **den** / **dem** Schrank. (*m.*)

9 Die Bäckerei steht zwischen **einem** / **einen** Supermarkt (*m.*) und einer / eine Post. (*f.*)

10 Das Flugzeug fliegt über **die** / **der** Stadt. (*f.*)

11 Ich stelle die Flaschen in **dem** / **den** Schrank. (*m.*)

12 Der Bus steht an **der** / **die** Haltestelle. (*f.*)

Some verbs work with a preposition which is followed by the accusative.

B Circle the correct article. Then translate the sentences into English.

1 Die Kinder streiten sich über **das** / **dem** Fernsehprogramm. (*n.*)

2 Wir freuen uns auf **das** / **dem** Festival. (*n.*)

3 Ich ärgere mich oft über **der** / **die** Arbeit. (*f.*)

4 Martin hat sich an **der** / **die** Sonne gewöhnt. (*f.*)

5 Wie lange warten Sie auf **der** / **die** Straßenbahn? (*f.*)

   1 ....

   2 ....

   3 ....

   4 ....

   5 ....

Certain special phrases have a preposition followed by either the accusative or the dative. You have to learn these.

C Draw lines to link the German and English phrases.

1 auf dem Land		*on the internet*
2 vor allem		*on the right*
3 auf die Nerven		*in the country*
4 auf der rechten Seite		*on my nerves*
5 im Internet		*above all*

89

Cases 3

Dieser (this) and *jener* (that) follow the pattern of *der, die, das*.

	m.	*f.*	*n.*	*pl.*
Nominative	dieser	diese	dieses	diese
Accusative	diesen	diese	dieses	diese
Dative	diesem	dieser	diesem	diesen

A Add the endings.

1 *this man*   dies........ Mann (*m.*)

2 *with this man*   mit dies........ Mann (*m.*)

3 *this woman*   dies........ Frau (*f.*)

4 *for this woman*   für dies........ Frau (*f.*)

5 *that horse*   jen........ Pferd (*n.*)

6 *on that horse*   auf jen........ Pferd (*n.*)

Kein, mein, dein, sein, ihr, unser, euer (eure) and *Ihr* follow the pattern of *ein*.

	m.	*f.*	*n.*	*pl.*
Nominative	kein	keine	kein	keine
Accusative	keinen	keine	kein	keine
Dative	keinem	keiner	keinem	keinen

B Complete the words where necessary with the correct ending.

1 Unser........ Schwester heißt Monika. (*f.*)

2 Ich habe kein........ Bruder. (*m.*)

3 Mein........ Schule ist nicht sehr groß. (*f.*)

4 Hast du dein........ Laptop vergessen? (*m.*)

5 Wie ist ihr........ Name, bitte? (*m.*)

6 Meine Lehrerin hat ihr........ Schulbücher nicht mit. (*pl.*)

7 Wo steht Ihr........ Auto? (*n.*)

8 Wir arbeiten in unser........ Büro. (*n.*)

9 Wo ist euer........ Wohnung? (*f.*)

10 Mein........ Lieblingsfächer sind Mathe und Informatik. (*pl.*)

11 Wie heißt dein........ Freundin? (*f.*)

12 Leider haben wir kein........ Zeit. (*f.*)

13 Ihr........ E-Mail war nicht sehr höflich. (*f.*)

14 Olaf geht mit sein........ Freund spazieren. (*m.*)

15 Madonna singt ihr........ besten Hits. (*pl.*)

16 Wo habt ihr euer........ Auto stehen lassen? (*n.*)

'Specials'

17 Ich habe .... Ahnung. (*I've no idea.*) (*f.*)

18 Ich habe .... Lust. (*I don't want to.*) (*f.*)

19 Das war .... Fehler. (*That was my mistake.*) (*m.*)

20 .... Meinung nach... (*In my opinion...*) (*f.*)

Adjective endings

Adjectives after the definite article end in either –e or –en.

	m.	f.	n.	pl.
Nominative	der kleine Hund	die kleine Maus	das kleine Haus	die kleinen Kinder
Accusative	den kleinen Hund	die kleine Maus	das kleine Haus	die kleinen Kinder
Dative	dem kleinen Hund	der kleinen Maus	dem kleinen Haus	den kleinen Kindern

A Fill the gaps with the suggested adjective and its correct ending.

1 Die .... Schülerin bekommt gute Noten. (f., intelligent__)

2 Wir fahren mit dem .... Bus in die Stadt. (m., nächst__)

3 Hast du den .... Vogel gesehen? (m., gelb__)

4 Der .... Lehrer ist streng. (m., altmodisch__)

5 Ich kaufe dieses .... Kleid. (n., schwarz__)

6 Die .... Reihenhäuser sind schön. (pl., neugebaut__)

7 Heute gehen wir in den .... Freizeitpark. (m., modern__)

8 Wir müssen dieses .... Fahrrad sauber machen. (n., schmutzig__)

9 Morgen gehen wir ins .... Einkaufszentrum. (n., neu__)

10 Der .... Zug kommt um ein Uhr an. (m., verspätet__)

Adjectives after the indefinite article have various endings. This also applies to *kein, mein, sein*, etc.

	m.	f.	n.	pl.
Nominative	ein kleiner Hund	eine kleine Maus	ein kleines Haus	meine kleinen Kinder
Accusative	einen kleinen Hund	eine kleine Maus	ein kleines Haus	meine kleinen Kinder
Dative	einem kleinen Hund	einer kleinen Maus	einem kleinen Haus	meinen kleinen Kindern

B Fill the gaps with the suggested adjective and its correct ending.

1 München ist eine .... Stadt. (f., umweltfreundlich__)

2 Ich suche ein .... T-Shirt. (n., preiswert__)

3 Marta hat ihre .... Handtasche verloren. (f., modisch__)

4 Wir haben unsere .... Hausaufgaben nicht gemacht. (pl., schwierig__)

5 Ich habe ein .... Bett gekauft. (n., bequem__)

6 Das ist ein .... Problem. (n., groß__)

7 Das war vielleicht eine .... Stunde! (f., langweilig__)

8 Diese .... Leute haben das Spiel verdorben. (pl., idiotisch__)

9 Mein Vater hat einen .... Unfall gehabt. (m., schwer__)

10 Klaus liebt seine .... Freundin. (f., neu__)

11 Wir haben kein .... Obst. (n., frisch__)

12 Maria hat einen .... Mantel gekauft. (m., grün__)

Comparisons

> To make comparisons between things, you use the comparative or superlative.
>
> Add –*er* for the comparative, or add –*(e)ste* for the superlative.
>
> Adjective: langsam – langsamer – langsamst- + ending (*slow, slower, slowest*)
>
> Adverb: langsam – langsamer – am langsamsten (*slowly, more slowly, most slowly*)

A Insert the comparative and superlative forms.

1 Mathe ist langweilig, Physik ist .... , aber das
.... Fach ist Kunst.

2 Oliver läuft schnell, Ali läuft .... , aber Tim läuft am
....

3 Berlin ist schön, Paris ist .... , aber Venedig ist die
.... Stadt.

4 Madonna ist cool, Lady Gaga ist .... , aber Beyoncé ist die
.... Sängerin.

5 Metallica ist .... als Guns 'n' Roses. (laut)

6 Bremen ist .... als Hamburg. (klein)

7 Deine Noten sind schlecht, aber meine sind noch ....

8 Ich finde Englisch .... als Französisch, aber Deutsch finde ich am
.... (einfach)

9 Skifahren ist .... als Radfahren. (schwierig)

10 Mein Auto ist .... als dein Auto, aber das Auto meines Vaters ist am
.... (billig)

> Some adjectives have small changes to the comparative and superlative forms.

B Fill in the gaps with the words provided below, then translate the sentences into English.

beste / länger / höher / besser / größer / jünger / am längsten

1 Ich bin .... als du. (jung)

2 Die Alpen sind .... als der Snowdon. (hoch)

3 München ist .... als der Bonn. (groß)

4 Meine Haare sind lang, Timos Haare sind .... , aber deine Haare sind
....

5 Fußball ist gut, Handball ist .... , aber Tennis ist das
.... Spiel.

1 ....

2 ....

3 ....

4 ....

5 ....

C Compare your likes and dislikes by using *gern*, *lieber* and *am liebsten*.

1 Ich spiele .... Korbball. (*like*)

2 Ich esse .... Gemüse als Fleisch. (*prefer*)

3 Am .... gehe ich schwimmen. (*like best*)

Personal pronouns

Like *der*, *die* and *das*, pronouns change depending on what case they are in: nominative, accusative or dative.

Nominative	Accusative	Dative
ich	mich	mir
du	dich	dir
er	ihn	ihm
sie	sie	ihr
es	es	ihm
wir	uns	uns
ihr	euch	euch
Sie/sie	Sie/sie	Ihnen/ihnen

A Use the correct pronoun in the appropriate case.

1 Ich liebe .... (*you, familiar*)

2 Liebst du .... ? (*me*)

3 Kommst du mit .... ? (*me*)

4 Mein Bruder ist nett. Ich mag .... gern. (*him*)

5 Ich habe keine Kreditkarte. Ich habe .... verloren. (*it*)

6 Ein Geschenk für .... ? Danke! (*us*)

7 Wir haben .... gestern gesehen. (*you, plural, familiar*)

8 Haben .... gut geschlafen? (*you, formal*)

9 Die Party ist bei .... (*me*)

10 Rolf hat Hunger. Ich bin mit .... essen gegangen. (*him*)

11 Vergiss .... nicht! (*me*)

12 Wie heißt .... ? (*you, familiar*)

13 Wie heißen .... ? (*you, formal*)

14 Meine Schwester ist krank. Gestern sind wir zu .... gegangen. (*her*)

15 Was ist los mit .... ? (*you, familiar*)

Certain special phrases use a dative pronoun.

es tut **mir** leid	*I am sorry*
es gefällt **ihm**	*he likes it*
es fällt **mir** schwer	*I find it difficult*
es geht **mir** gut	*I'm well*
es tut **ihr** weh	*it hurts her*
das schmeckt **mir**	*that tastes good*
das ist **mir** egal	*it's all the same to me*

B Fill in the gaps.

1 Schwimmen .... mir .... (= *I find it hard*)

2 Mmmm, Eis! .... es .... ? (= *do you [familiar] like the taste?/do you like it?*)

3 Aua! Das .... weh! (= *it hurts me*)

4 Leider .... es .... nicht gut. (= *we aren't well*)

5 Wer gewinnt im Fußball? Das .... (= *I don't care*)

6 Es .... leid. (= *we are sorry*)

Word order

> In German sentences, the **second** item is always the verb. In the perfect tense, the part of *haben* or *sein* comes in second position (see below).
>
> Daniel **fährt** in die Stadt.
> Morgen **fährt** Daniel in die Stadt.

A Rewrite these sentences with the new beginnings.

1 Die Fernsehsendung beginnt.

Um sechs Uhr ....

2 Ich fahre mit dem Bus zur Arbeit.

Jeden Tag ....

3 Meine Eltern sind krank.

Leider ....

4 Man darf nicht rauchen.

Hier ....

> In the perfect tense, the part of *haben* or *sein* comes in second position.
>
> Ich **bin** zum Jugendklub gegangen.
> Am Samstag **bin** ich zum Jugendklub gegangen.

B Now rewrite these sentences.

1 Wir haben Eis gegessen.

Gestern ....

2 Timo ist ins Kino gegangen.

Manchmal ....

3 Ali ist nach Frankreich gefahren.

Letztes Jahr ....

4 Du hast Pommes gekauft.

Heute Morgen ....

> Remember the word order in German: first **time**, then **manner**, then **place**.
>
>   **T**   **M**   **P**
> Ich spiele <u>jeden Tag</u> <u>mit meinem Bruder</u> <u>im Garten</u>.

C Write out these sentences in the right order.

1 jeden Tag / Ich fahre / zur Schule / mit dem Rad

....

2 am Wochenende / Gehst du / zum Schwimmbad? / mit mir

....

3 oft / fern / Wir sehen / im Wohnzimmer

....

4 Tischtennis / Mehmet spielt / im Jugendklub / abends

....

5 im Büro / Mein Vater arbeitet / fleißig / seit 20 Jahren

....

6 heute Abend / Willst du / Pizza essen? / im Restaurant / mit mir

....

Conjunctions

> The most common conjunction that introduces a subordinate clause is *weil* (because). It sends the verb to the end.
>
>   Ich gehe oft zu Partys, **weil** sie lustig sind.

A Join these sentences together using *weil*. Write the sentences out.

1 Claudia will Sportlehrerin werden. Sie ist sportlich.

....

2 Ich kann dich nicht anrufen. Ich habe mein Handy verloren.

....

3 Wir fahren nach Spanien. Das Wetter ist dort so schön.

....

4 Du darfst nicht im Garten spielen. Es regnet.

....

5 Peter hat seine Hausaufgaben nicht gemacht. Er ist faul.

....

6 Ich mag Computerspiele. Sie sind so aufregend.

....

> The following conjunctions also send the verb to the end: *als, bevor, bis, da, damit, dass, nachdem, ob, obwohl, während, was, wie, wenn*. In the perfect tense, the part of *haben* or *sein* comes last. In the future tense, it is *werden* that comes at the end.
>
>   Ich habe Golf gespielt, **während** du eingekauft hast.

B Join the sentences together using the conjunction indicated. Write the sentences out.

1 Du kannst abwaschen. Ich koche. (während)

....

2 Wir kaufen oft ein. Wir sind in der Stadt. (wenn)

....

3 Ich kann nicht zur Party kommen. Ich werde arbeiten. (da)

....

4 Lasst uns früh aufstehen. Wir können wandern. (damit)

....

5 Meine Eltern waren böse. Ich bin nicht spät nach Hause gekommen. (obwohl)

....

6 Ich habe es nicht gewusst. Du bist krank. (dass)

....

7 Papa hat geraucht. Er war jung. (als)

....

8 Ich weiß nicht. Man repariert einen Computer. (wie)

....

9 Wir können schwimmen gehen. Das Wetter ist gut. (wenn)

....

10 Wir müssen warten. Es regnet nicht mehr. (bis)

....

More on word order

> *um … zu* means 'in order to'. It needs an infinitive at the end of the clause.
>
>   Wir gehen in den Park, **um** Tennis **zu** spielen.

A Combine these sentences with *um … zu*.

1 Wir fahren in die Stadt. Wir kaufen Lebensmittel.

   ....

2 Viele Leute spielen Tennis. Sie werden fit.

   ....

3 Boris spart Geld. Er kauft ein Motorrad.

   ....

4 Meine Schwester geht zur Abendschule. Sie lernt Französisch.

   ....

5 Ich bin gestern zum Imbiss gegangen. Ich esse Pommes.

   ....

> There are some other expressions which use *zu* in the same way.

B Complete the sentences.

1 Das Orchester beginnt .... (*to play*)
2 Wir hoffen, ... (*to learn Spanish*)
3 Oliver versucht, ... (*to play guitar*)

> Relative pronouns, *der*, *die* or *das* (expressing 'who' or 'that' or 'which'), send the verb to the end of the clause.
>
>   das Mädchen, das krank ist   *the girl who is ill*

C Translate these expressions into German. You will find the expressions jumbled up in the box below.

1 the girl who plays tennis

   ....

2 the boy who sings well

   ....

3 the man who speaks German

   ....

4 the house (*n.*) that is old

   ....

5 the subject (*n.*) that is hard

   ....

6 the car (*n.*) that is broken

   ....

7 the cup (*f.*) that is full

   ....

das Auto,	das Fach,	der Deutsch spricht	das alt ist
der Junge,	das Mädchen,	das kaputt ist	das schwer ist
der Mann,	das Haus,	der gut singt	die voll ist
die Tasse,			das Tennis spielt

The present tense

> Verb endings in the present tense change according to who or what is doing the action.
>
> | ich | mach**e** | *I do/make* |
> | du | mach**st** | *you do/make* |
> | er / sie / es | mach**t** | *he/she/one does/makes* |
> | wir | mach**en** | *we do/make* |
> | ihr | mach**t** | *you do/make* |
> | Sie / sie | mach**en** | *they/you do/make* |

A Write in the correct form of the verb indicated. These verbs are all regular in the present tense.

    1 wir .... (*go*)

    2 er .... (*find*)

    3 sie .... (*sing*)

    4 ich .... (*play*)

    5 ihr .... (*do*)

    6 du .... (*say*)

    7 es .... (*come*)

    8 sie (*plural*) .... (*swim*)

    9 ich .... (*hear*)

    10 wir .... (*drink*)

> Some verbs have a vowel change in the *du* and *er/sie/es* forms of the present tense. Choose from those provided below.

B Insert the correct form of the present tense, then translate the sentences into English.

schläfst / fahrt / esst / isst / gibt / spricht / sprecht / nimmst / liest / lest / fährt / hilfst

    1 Was .... du? (lesen)

    2 .... du? (schlafen)

    3 Annabelle .... nicht gern Fleisch. (essen)

    4 Kerstin .... gut Englisch. (sprechen)

    5 .... du Zucker? (nehmen)

    6 Ben .... bald nach Berlin. (fahren)

    7 .... du mir, bitte? (helfen)

    8 Mein Onkel .... mir 20 Euro. (geben)

    ....

    ....

    ....

    ....

    ....

    ....

    ....

C Circle any irregular present tense verbs in this list.

    er spricht / du siehst / sie macht / es liegt / ich sage / sie fährt / du kommst / er liest

More on verbs

> Separable verbs have two parts: a prefix and the main verb. In a sentence, the prefix goes to the end.
>
>   einsteigen (*to get in*): Ich **steige** (*verb*) in das Taxi **ein** (*prefix*).

A Fill in the two gaps in these sentences.

1 Wir .... (abwaschen)

2 Er .... um 7 Uhr .... (aufwachen)

3 Wir .... oft Filme .... (herunterladen)

4 Wie oft .... du .... ? (fernsehen)

5 Wo .... man .... ? (aussteigen)

6 Ich .... nie .... (abwaschen)

> Separable verbs form the past participle as one word with the *ge-* in the middle: *ausgestiegen*.

B Put the above sentences into the perfect tense.

1 ....

2 ....

3 ....

4 ....

5 ....

6 ....

> Reflexive verbs are always used with a reflexive pronoun (*mich, dich, sich,* etc.).
>
>   Ich wasche **mich** im Badezimmer.
>
> | | |
> |---|---|
> | ich freue **mich** | wir freuen **uns** |
> | du freust **dich** | ihr freut **euch** |
> | er/sie/es freut **sich** | Sie/sie freuen **sich** |

C Fill in the correct reflexive pronoun, then translate the sentences into English.

1 Ich interessiere .... für Geschichte.

2 Sara freut .... auf die Ferien.

3 Erinnerst du .... an mich?

4 Wir langweilen .... in der Schule.

5 Ich habe .... noch nicht entschieden.

6 Dieter hat .... heute noch nicht rasiert.

7 Habt ihr .... gut amüsiert?

8 Unser Haus befindet .... in der Nähe vom Bahnhof.

1 ....

2 ....

3 ....

4 ....

5 ....

6 ....

7 ....

8 ....

Commands

> When telling someone what to do using the *Sie* (polite) form, swap the present tense round so the verb comes before the pronoun.
>
> Stehen Sie auf!

A Tell someone…

1 …not to park here. (parken)

....

2 …not to talk so loudly. (sprechen)

....

3 …to get off here. (aussteigen)

....

4 …not to drive so fast. (fahren)

....

5 …to come in. (hereinkommen)

....

6 …to go straight on. (gehen)

....

7 …to come back soon. (kommen)

....

8 …to give you 10 euros. (geben)

....

> When telling someone what to do using the *du* (familiar) form, use the present tense *du* form minus the *–st* ending.
>
> Steh auf!

B Tell a friend…

1 …to get up. (aufstehen)

....

2 …to write soon. (schreiben)

....

3 …to come here. (herkommen)

....

4 …to take two. (nehmen)

....

5 …to bring you the ball. (bringen)

....

6 …to stop. (aufhören)

....

7 …to behave. (sich benehmen)

....

8 …to sit down. (sich setzen)

....

Present tense modals

Modal verbs (*können, müssen, wollen, dürfen, sollen, mögen*) can't be used on their own. They need to be used with the infinitive of another verb at the end of the sentence.

A Write in the modal verb and the infinitive. Use words from the box below.

1 Ich .... nicht schnell .... (*can't run*)

2 Wir .... bald Kaffee .... (*must buy*)

3 Kinder .... keinen Alkohol .... (*shouldn't drink*)

4 Claudia .... nicht .... (*doesn't like to swim*)

5 Schüler .... hier nicht .... (*aren't allowed to sit*)

6 Wir .... Pommes .... (*want to eat*)

7 Hier .... man .... (*is allowed to park*)

8 Meine Eltern .... eine neue Wohnung .... (*want to buy*)

9 Du .... gut Fußball .... (*can play*)

10 Sie (*polite*) .... höflich .... (*should be*)

darf / dürfen / kann / kannst / müssen / sollten / sollten / mag / wollen / wollen
essen / kaufen / kaufen / laufen / parken / sein / sitzen / spielen / trinken / schwimmen

B Make these sentences into modal sentences, using the verbs provided.

Man trinkt nicht zu viel. ⟶ Man **soll** nicht zu viel **trinken**.

1 Im Kino raucht man nicht. (dürfen)

....

2 Wir gehen zur Bowlingbahn. (mögen)

....

3 Meine Freunde bleiben zu Hause. (wollen)

....

4 Ihr esst weniger. (müssen)

....

5 Man isst nicht viel Zucker. (sollen)

....

6 Ergül spielt gut Gitarre. (können)

....

7 Hilfst du mir mit meinen Hausaufgaben? (können)

....

8 Man betritt den Rasen nicht. (dürfen)

....

9 Wir fahren mit der Straßenbahn. (müssen)

....

10 Ich esse meinen Salat nicht. (wollen)

....

Imperfect modals

To use modals in the past, take the imperfect of the modal verb and the infinitive is sent to the end of the sentence.

müssen	muss**te**	*had to*
wollen	woll**te**	*wanted to*
dürfen	dur**fte**	*was allowed to*
sollen	soll**te**	*was supposed to*
mögen	moch**te**	*liked*
können	konn**te**	*was able to/could*

A Put these present modals into the imperfect.

   1 ich will ....

   2 wir müssen ....

   3 sie können ....

   4 sie darf ....

   5 man soll ....

   6 er mag ....

   7 wir wollen ....

   8 Jutta kann ....

B Put these modal sentences into the imperfect.

   Er kann gut singen. ⟶ Er **konnte** gut singen.

   1 Du sollst gesund essen.

   ....

   2 Wir müssen nach Hause gehen.

   ....

   3 Ella mag nicht Musik hören.

   ....

   4 Wir wollen im Internet surfen.

   ....

   5 Ich kann gut Tischtennis spielen.

   ....

   6 Ihr dürft spät ins Bett gehen.

   ....

Möchte (would like to) and *könnte* (could) are very useful forms. They also send the infinitive to the end.

C Translate these sentences.

   May I sit here? ⟶ Darf ich hier sitzen?

   1 Would you (*Sie*) like to play tennis?

   ....

   2 We could go shopping.

   ....

   3 I'd like to eat an ice cream.

   ....

   4 Could you (*du*) help me?

   ....

The perfect tense 1

Use the perfect tense to talk about something you have done in the past.

Form the perfect tense by using the verb *haben* plus the past participle at the end of the sentence.

Wir **haben** zu viel **gegessen**.

A Unjumble these perfect tense sentences.

1 Wir gespielt haben Minigolf.

....

2 gekauft ihr neue Habt Schuhe?

....

3 besucht du deine Hast Oma?

....

4 Was gesagt hat er?

....

5 habe Ich gelernt Spanisch.

....

6 Hast gelesen du Harry Potter?

....

7 ein Geschenk Dennis gegeben hat mir

....

8 gesehen einen haben tollen Wir Film.

....

Some verbs of movement use *sein* instead of *haben* to form the perfect tense.

B Insert the correct form of *sein* and a past participle.

1 Wohin .... du .... ? (fahren)

2 Wir .... nach Mallorca .... (fahren).

3 Ich .... zu Hause .... (bleiben)

4 Usain Bolt .... schnell .... (laufen)

5 Meine Mutter .... nach Amerika .... (fliegen)

6 Der Zug .... (abfahren)

C Circle the correct verb: *haben* or *sein*.

1 Abdul hat / ist 12 Stunden geschlafen.

2 Wir haben / sind unsere Hausaufgaben gemacht.

3 Wohin hast / bist du gefahren?

4 Ich habe / bin spät nach Hause gekommen.

5 Habt / Seid ihr Britta gesehen?

The perfect tense 2

> Many past participles are irregular and just have to be learnt.

A What are the past participles of these common verbs?

1	schwimmen	....	9	sprechen	....	
2	sein	....	10	treffen	....	
3	schließen	....	11	werden	....	
4	essen	....	12	trinken	....	
5	stehen	....	13	nehmen	....	
6	sitzen	....	14	singen	....	
7	schreiben	....	15	haben	....	
8	sterben	....				

B Now put these simple sentences into the perfect tense.

Wir sehen einen Film. ⟶ Wir **haben** einen Film **gesehen**.

1 Wir schreiben eine E-Mail.

....

2 Wir treffen uns um 6 Uhr.

....

3 Mein Onkel stirbt.

....

4 Nimmst du mein Handy?

....

5 Ich esse eine Bratwurst.

....

6 Er trinkt ein Glas Cola.

....

7 Wir schwimmen im Meer.

....

8 Marita spricht Italienisch.

....

> **(a)** Separable verbs add the *ge* between the prefix and the verb.
>
> einladen ⟶ ein**ge**laden
>
> **(b)** Verbs starting *be-*, *emp-*, *er-* or *ver-* don't add *ge* to the past participle.
>
> verstehen ⟶ verstanden

C Work out the past participles of these verbs.

1	vergessen	....	5	besuchen	....
2	aufstehen	....	6	herunterladen	....
3	empfehlen	....	7	abfahren	....
4	verlieren	....	8	aussteigen	....

The imperfect tense

> To form the imperfect (simple past) of regular verbs, take the *–en* off the infinitive, then add *t* and the ending.
>
> | | |
> |---|---|
> | ich hör**te** | *I heard/was hearing* |
> | du hör**test** | *you heard/were hearing* |
> | er / sie / man hör**te** | *he/she/one heard/was hearing* |
> | wir hör**ten** | *we heard/were hearing* |
> | ihr hör**tet** | *you heard/were hearing* |
> | Sie / sie hör**ten** | *you/they heard/were hearing* |

A Put these simple sentences into the imperfect.

Wir hören Musik. ⟶ Wir **hörten** Musik.

1 Ich spiele am Computer.

....

2 Was sagst du?

....

3 Nina kauft Kaugummi.

....

4 Die Schüler lernen Englisch.

....

5 Es schneit im Winter.

....

6 Peter lacht laut.

....

> *Haben* and *sein* have an irregular imperfect form: *hatte* and *war*, plus the appropriate endings.

B Fill the gaps with the imperfect tense of *sein* or *haben*.

1 Es .... gestern kalt.

2 Wir .... auf der Party viel Spaß.

3 Paul .... im Krankenhaus.

4 Meine Eltern .... drei Kinder.

5 Ich .... gestern im Imbiss.

6 .... du Angst?

> There are some irregular imperfect tense verbs which have to be learnt.

C Write **P** if the verb is in the present tense and **I** if it is in the imperfect.

1 Es gab viel zu essen.	....	7 Sie kamen um 6 Uhr an.	....
2 Wir sitzen im Kino.	....	8 Wie findest du das?	....
3 Es tut mir leid!	....	9 Aua! Das tat weh!	....
4 Ich fahre nach Berlin.	....	10 Ich fand es gut.	....
5 Er kommt früh an.	....	11 Es gibt nicht viel zu tun.	....
6 Er saß im Wohnzimmer.	....	12 Klaus fuhr zu schnell.	....

The future tense

> It is quite normal to use the present tense to indicate the future.
>
> Ich komme bald nach Hause.   *I'm coming home soon.*

A Use the present tense to indicate the future. Put the future expression straight after the verb.

Wir (gehen) einkaufen (morgen). ⟶ Wir gehen morgen einkaufen.

1 Susi (gehen) auf die Uni (nächstes Jahr).

....

2 Wir (fahren) nach Ibiza (im Sommer).

....

3 Er (kommen) zu uns (übermorgen).

....

4 Ich (bleiben) zu Hause (heute Abend).

....

5 (Bringen) du deine Schwester mit (am Wochenende)?

....

> To form the actual future tense, use the present tense of *werden* with the infinitive at the end of the sentence.
>
> | ich werde | wir werden |
> | --- | --- |
> | du wirst | ihr werdet |
> | er/sie/man wird | Sie/sie werden |

B Insert the correct form of *werden* and the appropriate infinitive from the box below.

Olaf **wird** Cola **trinken**.

1 Ich .... um 6 Uhr .... (*get up*)

2 .... du am Wochenende Musik .... ? (*listen*)

3 .... ihr Pizza .... ? (*eat*)

4 Wir .... die Prüfung .... (*pass*)

5 Nächstes Jahr .... wir nach Afrika .... (*travel*)

6 Daniel .... einen Film .... (*download*)

7 Ich .... ein Problem mit meinem Laptop .... (*have*)

8 Bayern München .... das Spiel .... (*win*)

9 Meine Freunde .... um 9 Uhr .... (*arrive*)

10 Meine Schwester .... im August .... (*get married*)

> heiraten / fahren / hören / essen / herunterladen / gewinnen / haben / ankommen / aufstehen / bestehen

C Write three true sentences about things you will do in the future.

1 ....

....

2 ....

....

3 ....

....

The conditional

> To form the conditional tense, use part of *würde* plus the infinitive at the end.
>
> | | |
> |---|---|
> | ich würde | wir würden |
> | du würdest | ihr würdet |
> | er/sie/man würde | Sie/sie würden |

A Fill in the correct part of *würde*.

1 Wenn wir Zeit hätten, ... wir einkaufen gehen.

2 Wenn meine Eltern Geld hätten, ... sie ein Auto kaufen.

3 Wenn ich Kinder hätte, ... ich sie lieben.

4 Wenn Tanja nicht krank wäre, ... sie Skateboard fahren.

5 Wenn du fleißiger wärst, ... du deine Prüfung bestehen.

6 Wenn das Wetter besser wäre, ... wir Sport treiben.

> The conditional of *haben* is *hätte*, with the appropriate endings. The conditional of *sein* is *wäre*, with the appropriate endings.

B Put in the right form of *hätte* or *wäre*.

1 Wenn ich Krankenschwester ...., würde ich mich freuen.

2 Wenn er Klempner ...., würde er viel verdienen.

3 Wenn wir in einer Fabrik arbeiten würden, ... wir müde.

4 Wenn wir Glasflaschen ...., würden wir sie recyceln.

5 Wenn ich Hunger ...., würde ich eine Bratwurst essen.

6 Wenn Manya und Timo Talent ...., würden sie in einer Band spielen.

> | | |
> |---|---|
> | ich möchte | *I would like* |
> | ich hätte gern | *I would like to have* |

C Write three sentences about things you would like to do. Start with *Ich möchte...*

1 ....

....

2 ....

....

3 ....

....

D Write three sentences about things you'd like to have. Start with *Ich hätte gern...*

1 ....

....

2 ....

....

3 ....

....

The pluperfect tense

> To form the pluperfect, (i.e. what *had* happened), use the imperfect form of **haben** or **sein** plus the past participle at the end.
>
> ich hatte (*I had, etc.*) wir hatten
> du hattest ihr hattet
> er/sie/man hatte Sie/sie hatten
>
> Ich **hatte** mein Buch vergessen. *I **had** forgotten my book.*

A Put in the right part of **haben** or **sein**, plus a past participle, to make these sentences pluperfect.

1 Wir .... Kaffee und Kuchen .... (*ordered*)

2 .... du Spaß .... ? (*had*)

3 Ich .... eine neue Stelle .... (*got*)

4 Wir .... unsere Freunde .... (*invited*)

5 Als ich nach Hause .... (*came*), habe ich gegessen.

6 Ergül .... zur Bäckerei .... (*gone*)

7 Sie (*plural*) .... zu Hause .... (*stayed*)

8 Ich .... mit dem Auto nach Frankfurt .... (*driven*)

B Write out these perfect tense sentences in the pluperfect. You only need to change the part of **haben** or **sein**.

1 Es ist nicht passiert.

....

2 Ich habe dir eine E-Mail geschickt.

....

3 Hast du dich nicht rasiert?

....

4 Ich bin sehr früh eingeschlafen.

....

5 Opa ist noch nie nach London gefahren.

....

6 Bist du zur Haltestelle gegangen?

....

7 Wir haben unseren Müll zur Mülldeponie gebracht.

....

8 Er hat zwei Computerspiele heruntergeladen.

....

9 Die Fabrik ist geschlossen worden.

....

10 Fatima hat Abitur gemacht.

....

Questions

To ask a simple question, just turn the pronoun (or name) and the verb around.

Du bist krank. ⟶ Bist du krank?

A Make these statements into questions.

1 Kevin spielt oft am Computer.

....

2 Du hast dein Handy verloren.

....

3 Wir wollen Volleyball spielen.

....

4 Hakan studiert Informatik.

....

5 Ihr geht morgen zum Sportzentrum.

....

B Ask the questions to which these are the answers.

Ja, ich habe Chips gekauft. ⟶ Hast du Chips gekauft?

1 Nein, ich bin nicht zum Supermarkt gefahren.

....

2 Ja, Ayse wird Chemie studieren.

....

3 Nein, mein Auto ist nicht kaputt.

....

4 Ja, ich esse gern Bratwurst mit Pommes.

....

5 Ich weiß nicht, ob es morgen regnen wird.

....

You have to learn the German question words.

C Draw lines to link the English and German question words.

who?	wessen?
what?	wie viele?
how?	warum?
when?	was für?
why?	wer?
where?	mit wem?
how many?	wie?
what kind of?	wann?
whose?	was?
who with?	wo?

D Write three questions you could ask an examiner during a speaking assignment.

1 ....

2 ....

3 ....

Time markers

Time markers are useful words for showing when something happens, did happen or will happen.

A Write what tense (present, past or future) these time markers indicate.

1 gestern ....
2 früher ....
3 bald ....
4 letzte Woche ....
5 heute ....

6 normalerweise ....
7 vor 2 Wochen ....
8 morgen ....
9 nächste Woche ....
10 jetzt ....

B Draw lines to link the English and German expressions.

manchmal	*immediately*
neulich	*on time*
sofort	*sometimes*
täglich	*in the future*
rechtzeitig	*recently*
in Zukunft	*every day*

C Rewrite these sentences using the time expressions provided. Put the time expression first and the verb second.

Wir fahren nach Bremen. (morgen) ⟶ Morgen fahren wir nach Bremen.

1 Ich werde mein Betriebspraktikum machen. (nächste Woche)

....

....

2 Ulli sieht fern. (heute Abend)

....

....

3 Man wird Strom sparen. (in Zukunft)

....

....

4 Du wirst einen Unfall haben. (bald)

....

....

5 Wir treffen uns mit unseren Freunden. (manchmal)

....

....

6 Ich war bei meinem Onkel. (neulich)

....

....

7 Mehmet hat sein Betriebspraktikum begonnen. (vorgestern)

....

....

8 Ich gehe zur Bäckerei. (jeden Tag)

....

....

Had a go ☐   Nearly there ☐   Nailed it! ☐

Numbers

Revise the numbers 1–1000. You need to be completely confident in using numbers.

A Write the German numbers in figures.

1 vierhunderteinundzwanzig   ....

2 tausendsechshundertvierundvierzig   ....

3 achtundsechzig   ....

4 dreihunderteins   ....

5 siebenundneunzig   ....

6 hundertfünf   ....

7 siebzehn   ....

8 sechshundertdreiundfünfzig   ....

B Write in the German numbers. Choose from the box below.

1 Es ist .... nach .... (20, 9)

2 Ausverkauf! .... Prozent Rabatt! (15)

3 Es ist .... Grad. (13)

4 Ich habe .... Euro gewonnen. (650)

5 Der Zug kommt um .... Minuten vor .... an. (12, 7)

6 Es gibt .... Schüler in meiner Klasse. (30)

sieben / zwölf / dreißig / fünfzehn / dreizehn / sechshundertfünfzig / neun / zwanzig

Revise the ordinal numbers.

1st	erste	20th	zwanzigste
2nd	zweite	21st	einundzwanzigste
3rd	dritte	30th	dreißigste
4th	vierte	31st	einunddreißigste
5th	fünfte		
6th	sechste		
7th	siebte		

C Write the dates in numbers.

        der einunddreißigste Mai ⟶ 31.5.

1 der zwölfte März   ....

2 der dreizehnte Juli   ....

3 der achtundzwanzigste Dezember ....

4 der erste April   ....

5 der dritte Januar   ....

6 der siebzehnte Juni   ....

D Write in the ordinal numbers.

1 Mein Geburtstag ist am .... November. (*1st*)

2 Saschas Geburtstag ist am .... September. (*7th*)

3 Das Konzert findet am .... Mai statt. (*12th*)

4 Die Ferien beginnen am .... Juli. (*2nd*)

Practice Exam Paper: Reading

Edexcel publishes official Sample Assessment Material on its website. This Practice Exam Paper has been written to help you practise what you have learned and may not be representative of a real exam paper.

Shopping

G

1 What is on the shopping list?

Write the correct letter in the box.

Example:	Present	E
(i)	Skirt	
(ii)	Stamps	
(iii)	Postcards	
(iv)	Camera	

Einkaufsliste

A Hose
B Briefmarken
C Fotoapparat
D Rock
E Geschenk
F Postkarten

(Total for Question 1 = 4 marks)

A restaurant review

E

2 Read this review about a new restaurant.

> Das neue griechische **Restaurant am Fluss** ist von 12:00 bis 20:30 Uhr geöffnet. Es ist sonntags geschlossen.
>
> Das Restaurant ist klein, aber man kann draußen oder drinnen sitzen. Das Tagesgericht ist billig, aber die anderen Gerichte auf der Speisekarte sind ziemlich teuer. Der Schweinebraten schmeckt sehr gut.
>
> Man muss ziemlich lange warten, aber die Kellner sind sehr freundlich.

Complete the details about the new restaurant. Write the correct letter.

A Monday   F cheap

B friendly   G tasty

C expensive   H Greek

D Sunday   I disgusting

E funny

> Don't just go for the first word you recognise. Look carefully at the choices.

Example: Type of restaurant ....H......... .

(i) The restaurant is closed on ....

(ii) The dish of the day is ....

(iii) The pork is ....

(iv) The waiters are ....

(Total for Question 2 = 4 marks)

Signs around town

F 3 Look at these signs.

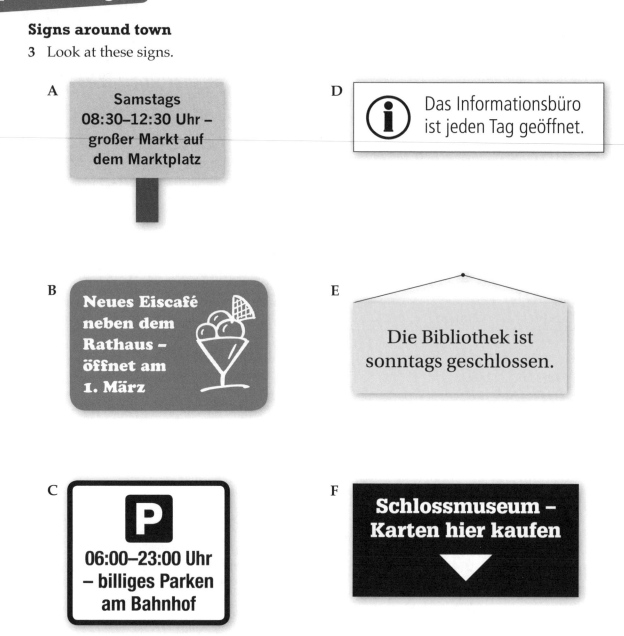

A
Samstags
08:30–12:30 Uhr –
großer Markt auf
dem Marktplatz

D
(i) Das Informationsbüro
ist jeden Tag geöffnet.

B
Neues Eiscafé
neben dem
Rathaus –
öffnet am
1. März

E
Die Bibliothek ist
sonntags geschlossen.

C
P
06:00–23:00 Uhr
– billiges Parken
am Bahnhof

F
Schlossmuseum –
Karten hier kaufen
▼

Which sign is it? Put a cross in the correct box.

Look for key words.

	A	**B**	**C**	**D**	**E**	**F**
Example: New café opening		X				
(i) Cheap parking						
(ii) Where to buy tickets						
(iii) Open every day						
(iv) Closed on Sundays						

(Total for Question 3 = 4 marks)

My family

4 Read Mina's email.

> Ich habe einen kleinen Bruder. Er heißt Tom und ist fünf Jahre alt. Er ist oft sehr laut!
>
> Mein Vater ist sehr lustig. Er hat braune Haare und grüne Augen. Meine Mutter ist hübsch und hat lockige Haare. Sie ist sehr nett.

Toolbar: Löschen | Antworten | Antworten Alle | Weiher | Drueken

Answer the questions in **English.**

Example: What is Mina's brother called? .....Tom...

(a) How old is Mina's brother? .... **(1 mark)**

(b) What is he often like? .... **(1 mark)**

(c) What is her father like? .... **(1 mark)**

(d) What is her mother's hair like? .... **(1 mark)**

(Total for Question 4 = 4 marks)

Hotel reviews

5 Read visitors' comments about hotels.

Comments

A   Das Hotel liegt am Fluss und es gibt keinen Lärm. Man kann sich gut ausruhen und draußen sitzen oder lesen.

B   Ein bequemes Hotel. In der Nähe gibt es interessante Museen und Galerien. Das alte Schloss ist besonders schön.

C   Es gibt nur acht Zimmer in diesem freundlichen Hotel. Kinder und ihre Eltern sind sehr willkommen und im Erdgeschoss gibt es ein Spielzimmer mit Fernsehapparat.

D   Ein tolles Hotel. Die Zimmer sind sehr groß und das Essen im Restaurant ist fantastisch.

E   Das Hotel ist nicht weit von der Stadtmitte entfernt, wo es tolle Klubs und Cafés für Jugendliche gibt.

F   Alle Zimmer im ersten Stock haben eine schöne Aussicht auf den See, wo man Wassersport treiben kann. Es gibt auch Tennisplätze.

Which hotel is it? Put a cross in the correct box.

Which hotel is good for…

		A	B	C	D	E	F
Example:	sporty people?						X
(i)	families?						
(ii)	people wanting peace and quiet?						
(iii)	sightseeing visitors?						
(iv)	young people?						

(Total marks for Question 5 = 4)

Part-time jobs

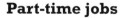

6 Read this article.

> Richard hat schon ein paar Nebenjobs gemacht.
>
> Seit Januar arbeitet er am Wochenende in einem Freizeitzentrum und das macht ihm viel Spaß. Als er jünger war, hat er jeden Tag Zeitungen ausgetragen, aber er hat nicht viel verdient.
>
> In den Sommerferien wird Richard als Kellner in einem Café in der Stadtmitte arbeiten. Er ist sehr froh, weil der Job gut bezahlt wird. Er hilft sehr gern im Schnellimbiss im Freizeitzentrum aus, aber er braucht mehr Geld.
>
> Er hat auch drei Monate in einer Bäckerei gearbeitet, aber er fand es schlecht, weil der Chef sehr streng war.

Do the activities belong in the past, present or future?

Put a cross in the **four** correct boxes.

		Past	Present	Future
Example:	Working in a leisure centre.		X	
(a)	Delivering newspapers.			
(b)	Having a well-paid job.			
(c)	Helping in a snack bar.			
(d)	Having a strict boss.			

(Total for Question 6 = 4 marks)

In a youth club

7 Read these comments.

> *Sophie*: Es gibt viel zu tun. Manchmal sehen wir Filme und das macht viel Spaß.
>
> *Esma*: Ich liebe Musik. Im Klub lerne ich, Schlagzeug zu spielen. Am Freitag spielen wir auf einem Konzert.
>
> *Hanna*: Im Moment machen wir einen kurzen Dokumentarfilm über den Klub und das ist wirklich interessant.
>
> *Adam*: Am See können wir angeln und ich finde das viel besser als Schwimmen.
>
> *Mehmet*: Ich kann mit anderen Jungen und Mädchen plaudern oder Musik hören.
>
> *Ben*: Ab und zu können wir warmes Essen kochen, und dann essen wir zusammen. Letzte Woche habe ich mit drei Freunden Nudeln gekocht.

Who says what? Put the correct name in the box.

We can…

Example:	…go fishing.	Adam
(a)	…play a musical instrument.	
(b)	…make a meal.	
(c)	…chat to other young people.	
(d)	…make a film.	

(Total for Question 7 = 4 marks)

A visit to an English school

A

8 You read this article.

> Vor drei Wochen sind zwanzig Schüler aus Bonn nach England gefahren, weil sie ihre englischen Sprachkenntnisse verbessern wollten. Um Geld zu sparen, haben sie in einer Jugendherberge in London übernachtet.
>
> Jeder Schüler muss jetzt einen Aufsatz über englische Schulen schreiben. Sie haben also eine Gesamtschule besucht und waren besonders froh, dass der Schultag später angefangen hat. Eine halbe Stunde länger im Bett ist immer gut!
>
> Die Schüler hatten nicht gewusst, dass man in England nicht sitzen bleiben muss. Sie finden, das ist eine gute Idee, aber sie wollen keine Versammlungen in ihrer Realschule haben. Sie fanden die Schuluniform praktisch und ein Junge hat sogar einen Schulpullover als Souvenir gekauft.
>
> Sie waren ein bisschen nervös, als sie in der Deutschstunde über deutsche Schulen sprechen mussten, aber die englischen Schüler haben viele Fragen gestellt..

Answer the questions in **English.**

(a) Why did the visit take place?

.... **(1 mark)**

(b) Why did they stay in a youth hostel?

.... **(1 mark)**

(c) What must the students do now?

.... **(1 mark)**

(d) Why did they like starting school later?

.... **(1 mark)**

(e) What surprised them about English schools?

.... **(1 mark)**

(f) How do they feel about having assemblies in their school?

.... **(1 mark)**

(g) What did one student do?

.... **(1 mark)**

(h) What were they worried about?

.... **(1 mark)**

(Total for Question 8 = 8 marks)

Sport

A* 9 Read Hanna's blog.

> Ich bin Sportfanatikerin! Ich sehe gern Sport im Fernsehen. Manchmal gehe ich am Samstag mit meinem Vater ins Fußballstadion, und das finde ich noch besser. Aber am liebsten treibe ich Sport, weil ich fit bleiben will. Außerdem macht es mir viel Spaß.
>
> Seit sechs Jahren ist Leichtathletik mein Sport Nummer eins. Am Anfang habe ich zweimal pro Woche trainiert, aber jetzt mache ich viel mehr. Dienstags und donnerstags stehe ich früh auf, um vor der Schule zu joggen. Samstags und sonntags muss ich im Stadion weiter trainieren. Es ist ermüdend, aber es ist nötig, weil ich bei den Meisterschaften gewinnen will.
>
> Um mich zu relaxen, gehe ich mindestens einmal pro Woche mit Freunden schwimmen. Mein Vater holt mich danach ab, aber er schwimmt nicht. Im Sommer fahren wir zum Freibad in der nächsten Stadt.
>
> Als ich letzten April meine Freundin in London besucht habe, hatten wir Karten für ein Rugbyspiel im Stadion in Twickenham. Das Spiel war sehr spannend, aber ich fand die Regeln ziemlich kompliziert. Leichtathletik ist viel leichter!

A Put a cross in the correct box.

> You can double check your correct answer by knowing why the other two are wrong.

Example: Hanna findet Sport im Fernsehen…

(i)	besser als ein Spiel im Stadion.	
(ii)	besser als Sport treiben.	
(iii)	sehr gut.	X

(a) Hannas Lieblingssport ist…

(i)	Fußball.	
(ii)	Leichtathletik.	
(iii)	Schwimmen.	

(c) Hanna geht jede Woche…

(i)	alleine schwimmen.	
(ii)	mit anderen schwimmen.	
(iii)	mit ihrem Vater schwimmen.	

(b) Hanna trainiert Leichtathletik…

(i)	zweimal pro Woche.	
(ii)	nur am Wochenende.	
(iii)	in der Woche und am Wochenende.	

(d) Hanna findet die Rugbyregeln…

(i)	schwer zu verstehen.	
(ii)	leicht zu verstehen.	
(iii)	leichter als Leichtathletik.	

B Put a cross next to the **four** correct statements.

Example:	Hanna schaut gern Sport.	X
(a)	Hanna ist nicht sehr sportlich.	
(b)	Sie will in Form bleiben.	
(c)	Sie trainiert ab und zu.	
(d)	Sie joggt jeden Tag vor der Schule.	
(e)	Sie will in Leichtathletik Erfolg haben.	
(f)	Sie findet Schwimmen entspannend.	
(g)	Sie geht jede Woche ins Freibad.	
(h)	Sie fand das Rugbyspiel langweilig.	

(Total for Question 9 = 8 marks)

Practice Exam Paper: Listening

Edexcel publishes official Sample Assessment Material on its website. This Practice Exam Paper has been written to help you practise what you have learned and may not be representative of a real exam paper.

Clothes

G 1 What are they wearing? Listen and put a cross in the correct box.

Example:

(i)	Trousers.	X
(ii)	Shirt.	
(iii)	Jacket.	

(1)

(i)	Dress.	
(ii)	Blouse.	
(iii)	Skirt.	

(3)

(i)	Jumper.	
(ii)	Dress.	
(iii)	Blouse.	

(2)

(i)	Shorts.	
(ii)	Tie.	
(iii)	Jacket.	

(4)

(i)	Jeans.	
(ii)	Shirt.	
(iii)	Jumper.	

(Total for Question 1 = 4 marks)

At school

F 2 Petra is talking about school. Listen and put a cross in the correct box.

Example: She goes to school by…

(i)	bus.	
(ii)	bike.	X
(iii)	car.	

(1) She likes…

(i)	Art.	
(ii)	Maths.	
(iii)	English.	

(3) School finishes at…

(i)	1.30 p.m.	
(ii)	1.00 p.m.	
(iii)	2.00 p.m.	

(2) Her favourite day is…

(i)	Monday.	
(ii)	Thursday.	
(iii)	Friday.	

(4) After school she…

(i)	plays badminton.	
(ii)	goes swimming.	
(iii)	plays football.	

(Total for Question 2 = 4 marks)

117

At the market

E

3 Olga is at the market. Which fruit and vegetables does she buy?

Listen and put a cross in the **four** correct boxes.

A Pineapple	B Strawberries	C Carrots	D Beans
		X	
E Potatoes	F Apples	G Onions	H Bananas

(Total for Question 3 = 4 marks)

Directions

D

4 Leona is asking for directions. Listen and put the correct letter in each box.

A
in front of the
department store

D
16.30

G
straight on

B
15 minutes

E
cathedral

H
in front of the
town hall

C
right

F
17.30

I
30 minutes

Example: Leona wants to go to the ☐E☐ .

(i) The tram stop is ☐ and ☐ .

(ii) The trams run every ☐ .

(iii) The next one is due at ☐ .

> Look carefully at each option and think about which ones would make sense in each sentence, before you listen.

(Total for Question 4 = 4 marks)

At the doctor's

5 Why are these people visiting the doctor? Listen and put a cross in the correct box.

	Jonas	Martha	Benjamin	Danni	Kevin
Example: Headache	X				
(i) Sore back					
(ii) Feverish					
(iii) Sore leg					
(iv) Cough					

(Total for Question 5 = 4 marks)

A guest house booking

6 The Deinhardt family are going to Germany and Mrs Deinhardt telephones the bed and breakfast to confirm her booking.

Listen and complete the sentences by putting a cross in the correct box.

Example: The booking is for…

(i)	next week.	X
(ii)	tomorrow.	
(iii)	next month.	

(a) Mrs Deinhardt is ringing because…

(i)	she wants to book a single room.	
(ii)	there will be one person fewer in her group.	
(iii)	she wants to change the date of arrival.	

(b) Mrs Deinhardt's rooms…

(i)	have a balcony.	
(ii)	look on to the river.	
(iii)	look on to a park.	

(c) The Deinhardt family will be arriving…

(i)	early morning.	
(ii)	early evening.	
(iii)	late at night.	

(d) The family…

(i)	have never visited the area before.	
(ii)	visited the area last year.	
(iii)	normally come to this area.	

(Total for Question 6 = 4 marks)

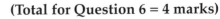

119

Weekends

7   Felix describes his weekend. What did he do last weekend and what are his plans for next weekend? Listen and put the correct letter in each box.

A | shopping
D | playing chess

B | staying at home
E | watching a game

C | playing hockey
F | watching a film

Last weekend	Next weekend
Example: B	–
(i)	**(iii)**
(ii)	**(iv)**

(Total for Question 7 = 4 marks)

My best friend

8   Rene is talking about her best friend, Sandra.
     What does she say?

Listen and put a cross in the **four** correct boxes.

Example:	Rene met her on holiday.	X
(a)	Sandra is very different to Rene.	
(b)	The two girls have much in common.	
(c)	Sandra is good looking.	
(d)	Sandra is cheerful.	
(e)	Sandra is selfish.	
(f)	Sandra is generous.	
(g)	Sandra is shy.	
(h)	Sandra can be annoying.	

(Total for Question 8 = 4 marks)

Zell am See

A

9 The tourist office manager, Frau Juric, is talking about Zell am See. Listen and answer the questions in **English**.

(a) What has Zell am See been famous for since 1928?

.... **(1 mark)**

(b) Name two key attractions for winter guests.

(i) .... **(1 mark)**

(ii) .... **(1 mark)**

(c) Who in particular might like to visit Zell am See in the summer?

.... **(1 mark)**

(Total for Question 9 = 4 marks)

Shopping

A*

10 Nadine describes a recent problem she had with shopping. What does she say?

Listen and put a cross in the **four** correct boxes.

(a)	Nadine went shopping with her cousin.	
(b)	She was shopping for her cousin's birthday party.	
(c)	On the journey home Nadine noticed the dress had a fault.	
(d)	Nadine didn't notice the dress was faulty till she got home.	
(e)	Nadine didn't have the receipt.	
(f)	Nadine exchanged it for another dress.	
(g)	Nadine has got some shoes to match the outfit.	
(h)	The new outfit does not go with any of Nadine's shoes.	

(Total for Question 10 = 4 marks)

Answers

Personal information

1 **(a)** David **(b)** Marie
   (c) Julia **(d)** Frank

2 **(a)** Markus **(b)** Mr Schulz
   (c) Sabine **(d)** Mrs Schulz

3 **(i)** H **(ii)** F **(iii)** D **(iv)** I

4 **(a)** short **(b)** quite tall
   (c) 16 **(d)** glasses

5 (a) (c) (d) (h)

6 **(i)** C **(ii)** A **(iii)** B **(iv)** B

7 **(a)** Elias **(b)** Susi
   (c) Leila **(d)** Maria

8 **(a)** Freddy **(b)** — **(c)** Freddy
   (d) Hannes **(e)** Freddy

9 A C D G

10 **(a) (i)** lively / always something to do
        for children and adults
     (ii) public transport excellent and
        good value for money
    (b) (i) bigger house (with a view)
     (ii) need a (second) car

11 **(i)** I **(ii)** H **(iii)** B **(iv)** F

12 **(i)** A **(ii)** H **(iii)** D **(iv)** C

13 **(a) (ii)** A **(iii)** D **(iv)** F **(v)** C
    (b) (i) (iv) (v) (viii)

14 **(a)** Max **(b)** Ahmed
    (c) Hanna **(d)** Lena

15 **(i)** E **(ii)** A **(iii)** F **(iv)** D

16 **(a)** Ali **(b)** Fabian
    (c) Teresa **(d)** Adam

17 **(i)** E **(ii)** B **(iii)** A **(iv)** C

18 C D E H

19 **(a)** Julia **(b)** Julia **(c)** Gabi
    (d) — **(e)** Julia

20 **(a)** Sara **(b)** Maria
    (c) Adam **(d)** Ralf

21 **(i)** A **(ii)** C **(iii)** B **(iv)** A

22 **(a)** (ii) **(b)** (iii) **(c)** (ii) **(d)** (iii)

23 **(i)** F **(ii)** A **(iii)** E **(iv)** C

24 (a) (b) (e) (g)

25 **(a)** Sofia **(b)** Luca
    (c) Felix **(d)** Lena

26 **(a)** adventure film
    (b) the mountains / the Himalayas
    (c) become good friends
    (d) Germany too warm
    (e) whole family
    (f) one / it's her first film
    (g) better than adults
    (h) film in German

27 **(a)** opposite the town hall
    (b) cousin recommended it
    (c) was romantic and funny
    (d) special offer / only €11 for ticket, 3D
        glasses and a drink

28 **(a)** Germany **(b)** 2004
    (c) German **(d)** radio

29 **(a)** Anja **(b)** Jessica
    (c) Anja **(d)** Jessica

30 **(a)** school work **(b)** get cross
    (c) chats with friends **(d)** expensive
    (e) it's practical / you can quickly see
        which films are on and what people
        recommend **(f)** shops for clothes
    (g) (i) emails friends
     (ii) reads news / sports reports

31 **(i)** A **(ii)** E **(iii)** B **(iv)** C

32 **(a)** (ii) **(b)** (iii) **(c)** (i) **(d)** (iii)

33 **(a)** Leila **(b)** Felix
    (c) Ahmed **(d)** Felix

34 **(i)** H, F **(ii)** B **(iii)** D

35 **(a)** (i) **(b)** (iii) **(c)** (i) **(d)** (ii)

36 **(a)** (ii) **(b)** (i) **(c)** (iii) **(d)** (iii)

37 **(a)** Adam **(b)** Tom
    (c) Ben **(d)** Mina

38 (b) (d) (f) (h)

39 **(a)** (iii) **(b)** (i) **(c)** (i **(d)** (iii)
    (e) (i) **(f)** (iii) **(g)** (ii) **(h)** (iii)

40 **(a)** Ali **(b)** Fabian
    (c) Teresa **(d)** Adam

41 **(i)** D **(ii)** C **(iii)** F **(iv)** B

42 **(i)** Mehmet **(ii)** Ralf
    (iii) Adam **(iv)** Maria

43 **(a)** (iii) **(b)** (ii) **(c)** (ii) **(d)** (ii)

Out and about

1 (i) G   (ii) I   (iii) E   (iv) H

2 (a) (ii)   (b) (i)   (c) (iii)   (d) (ii)

3 (a) go back / visit again
   (b) North Germany
   (c) book in advance
   (d) (i) cheaper fares
      (ii) price reduction on theatre, tours, etc. / reductions on other things
   (e) (i) shop / buy souvenirs or presents
      (ii) try food specialities
   (f) on Mondays

4 (i) B   (ii) F   (iii) C   (iv) E

5 (a) tourists
   (b) Either: on (all) public transport (in the town) or: in the whole town / in all of Berlin / throughout the city NOT in town on its own / in towns
   (c) children under 6
   (d) at the station / at the airport

6 (i) F   (ii) C   (iii) A   (iv) E

7 (i) D   (ii) B   (iii) A   (iv) E

8 (i) D   (ii) A   (iii) F   (iv) C

9 (i) B   (ii) A   (iii) D   (iv) E

10 B C G I

11 (i) E   (ii) D   (iii) F   (iv) A

12 (b) (e) (f) (h)

13 (i) A   (ii) F   (iii) D   (iv) E

14 (a) Sophie   (b) Felix
   (c) Lilli   (d) Felix

15 **A**
   (a) a shopping centre
   (b) industry has been replaced by museums
   (c) rural and flat
   (d) he likes it
   B
   (a) it's difficult
   (b) the people have left / no one lives there any more
   (c) he never sees a good game / match
   (d) leave the town / live somewhere else

16 **A** (a) (i)   (b) (i)   (c) (ii)   (d) (iii)
   B (a) (b) (e) (f)

17 (a) Leon   (b) Anna
   (c) Ben   (d) Anna

18 (i) A   (ii) C   (iii) E   (iv) F

19 (a) (iii)   (b) (ii)   (c) (i)   (d) (i)

20 (i) C   (ii) D   (iii) E   (iv) A

21 (a) (c) (e) (g)

22 The bathrooms – good
The bedrooms – bad
The living room – good
The heating – bad

23 (a) 18   (b) ground floor
   (c) disco   (d) car park

24 (i) A   (ii) F   (iii) H   (iv) I

25 (b) (e) (g) (h)

26 Likes: A and D   Dislikes: F and G

27 (i) F   (ii) B   (iii) E   (iv) A

28 Patricia: C, D   Manuela: A, F

29 (a) have fun / relax
   (b) like warmer weather
   (c) at the seaside / on the coast
   (d) (i) swim
      (ii) lie on a beach / play volleyball / football
   (e) go to bed late / stay up late
   (f) visit sights / visit castles and old churches
   (g) it's boring

30 (a) 11th August   (b) 4
   (c) bath   (d) town map

31 (a) (iii)   (b) (i)   (c) (ii)   (d) (ii)

32 (b) (d) (f) (g)

33 (b) (e) (f) (h)

34 (a) (iii)   (b) (ii)   (c) (i)
   (d) (iii)   (e) (i)   (f) (ii)
   (g) (iii)   (h) (ii)

35 (i) F   (ii) D   (iii) A   (iv) G

36 (i) F   (ii) C   (iii) A   (iv) B

37 (i) F   (ii) A   (iii) E   (iv) C

38 (i) C   (ii) A   (iii) D   (iv) B

39 (i) I   (ii) F   (iii) C   (iv) E

40 (a) (i)   (b) (iii)   (c) (ii)   (d) (iii)

Customer service and transactions

1 C E F G

2 **(i)** F   **(ii)** C   **(iii)** E   **(iv)** B

3 **(a)** friendly   **(b)** young (people)
   (c) fantastic / great   **(d)** expensive

4 **(a)** Susanne   **(b)** Michael
   (c) Michael   **(d)** —   **(e)** Susanne

5 **(a)** Daniel   **(b)** Johannes
   (c) Tom   **(d)** Anna

6 **(i)** A   **(ii)** F   **(iii)** D   **(iv)** C

7 **(b)** **(d)** **(f)** **(h)**

8

	Matthias	Eva
Example: Starter	X	
Fish		X
Pork	X	
Dessert	X	
Drinks		X

9 **(a)** Ali   **(b)** Adam
   (c) Leila   **(d)** Jacob

10 **(a)** (iii)   **(b)** (iii)   **(c)** (ii)   **(d)** (ii)

11 **(a)** last night / yesterday evening
   (b) Sara's / her mother's birthday
   (c) a month ago
   (d) next to toilets
   (e) find another table
   (f) **(i)** vegetarian main meals were cold
        (ii) not much fruit on fruit flan
   (g) go back (to restaurant)

12 **(i)** C   **(ii)** A   **(ii)** F   **(iv)** D

13 **A Leon**
   (a) to get a present for his mother's
        birthday
   (b) **(i)** a large selection
        (ii) it is cheap
   (c) a TV set

   B Maria
   (a) she needs them for different occasions
        (anything along those lines, e.g. for
        school and job)
   (b) looks at all the clothes and chooses
        some
   (c) trying on clothes
   (d) whenever she has any money left

14 **(a)** a kilo   **(b)** small
   (c) a cauliflower   **(d)** strawberries

15 **(a)** peaches   **(b)** potatoes
   (c) 70 cents   **(d)** half a kilo (one pound)

16 **(b)** **(e)** **(f)** **(h)**

17 **(a)** (ii)   **(b)** (i)   **(c)** (iii)   **(d)** (ii)

18 **(a)** future   **(b)** past
   (c) past   **(d)** future

19 **(a)** (i)   **(b)** (ii)   **(c)** (iii)   **(d)** (iii)

20 **(i)** E   **(ii)** A   **(iii)** F   **(iv)** D

21 **(a)** (i)   **(b)** (iii)   **(c)** (ii)   **(d)** (ii)

22 **(i)** E   **(ii)** A   **(iii)** F   **(iv)** B

23 **(i)** D   **(ii)** B   **(iii)** E   **(iv)** C

24 **(i)** D   **(ii)** E   **(iii)** B   **(iv)** F

25 **(i)** D   **(ii)** C   **(iii)** B   **(iv)** B

26 **(i)** C   **(ii)** B   **(iii)** D   **(iv)** F

27 **(i)** D   **(ii)** B   **(iii)** C   **(iv)** H

28 **(a)** lots of different products
   (b) **(i)** lots / hundreds of ideas
        (ii) branded goods at great prices /
             cheap branded goods
   (c) can't try on before you buy
   (d) look in shops first
   (e) **(i)** saves time
        (ii) don't need to leave the house
   (f) shopping arrives late or fruit and veg
        not fresh

29 **(a)** (iii)   **(b)** (i)   **(c)** (i)
   (d) (iii)   **(e)** (iii)   **(f)** (i)
   (g) (i)   **(h)** (iii)

30 **(i)** D   **(ii)** E   **(iii)** A   **(iv)** B

31 **(b)** **(c)** **(e)** **(g)**

32 **(a)** April   **(b)** €20 or identity card
   (c) a present   **(d)** brochure

33 **(b)** **(e)** **(f)** **(h)**

34 **(a)** Fatima   **(b)** Max
   (c) Ben   **(d)** Adam

35 **(a)** **(c)** **(e)** **(h)**

36 **(b)** **(c)** **(e)** **(h)**

37 **(i)** A   **(ii)** C   **(iii)** E   **(iv)** F

38 **A** **(a)** (iii)   **(b)** (ii)
      (c) (i)   **(d)** (ii)
   B (a) (d) (g) (h)

Future plans, education and work

1 **(i)** A **(ii)** C **(iii)** F **(iv)** B
2 **(i)** Ilayda D German
 (ii) Celina B Geography
 (iii) Romeo A Physics
 (iv) Eva C Art
3 **(a)** (i) **(b)** (ii) **(c)** (i) **(d)** (ii)
4 (a) (d) (e) (g)
5 (a) (c) (e) (g)
6 **(i)** E **(ii)** A **(iii)** B **(iv)** F
7 (b) (c) (e) (g)
8 **(a) (i)** it was quiet
 (ii) she could wear what she liked
 (b) (i) good selection of clubs
 (ii) tiring as get home at six after
 clubs / school day finishes at 3.20
9 **(a)** Ben **(b)** Eric
 (c) Lena **(d)** Susi
10 **(i)** A **(ii)** F **(iii)** D **(iv)** E
11 **(i)** E **(ii)** A **(iii)** F **(iv)** B
12 **(a)** (iii) **(b)** (ii) **(c)** (ii) **(d)** (i)
13 **(a)** her last exam
 (b) best in the area
 (c) chill/relax with friends in Spain
 (d) next year will be hard work
 (e) decided to work with animals
 (f) study to be a vet
 (g) in a different town
 (h) work with animals in Africa
14 **A (a)** (i) **(b)** (ii)
 (c) (iii) **(d)** (i)
 B (a) (c) (f) (g)
15 (b) (e) (g) (h)
16 **(i)** Philipp D **(ii)** Özlem B
 (iii) Christoph A **(iv)** Gerhard E
17 **(a)** hard-working / friendly
 (b) waiter
 (c) 12.00/midday
 (d) €8.50

18 **(i)** D **(ii)** G **(iii)** B **(iv)** E, C
19 **(i)** F **(ii)** C **(iii)** E **(iv)** H
20 **(a)** 17 **(b)** grammar school
 (c) hospital **(d)** intelligent/clever
21 **(a)** past **(b)** present
 (c) past **(d)** future
22 **(i)** B **(ii)** C **(iii)** D **(iv)** F
23 **(a)** (iii) **(b)** (ii) **(c)** (ii) **(d)** (iii)
24 **(a)** Ozan **(b)** Susi
 (c) Jan **(d)** Lina
25 **(a)** stand outside the changing room
 (b) shouted at sales assistants
 (c) 30 days' holiday per year and 10%
 discount in all departments
26 **(a)** paper round / delivers papers
 (b) getting up early
 (c) gets tired (in the evening) / it's tiring
 (d) working on the till
 (e) in a Turkish restaurant / his uncle's
 restaurant
 (f) works as a waiter
 (g) being outside
 (h) wants to be a gardener
27 **(a)** shop **(b)** 8
 (c) nice **(d)** great
28 (b) (d) (e) (h)
29 **(a) (ii)** F **(iii)** A **(iv)** D **(v)** E
 (b) (i) (iv) (vi) (viii)
30 **(i)** Sandra **(ii)** Kevin
 (iii) Fransiska **(iv)** Jana
31 **(a)** (ii) **(b)** (i) **(c)** (ii) **(d)** (iii)
32 **(i)** C **(ii)** A **(iii)** E **(iv)** B
33 **(i)** F **(ii)** D **(iii)** A **(iv)** C
34 **(a)** Lara **(b)** Adam
 (c) Tom **(d)** Lilli
35 **(a)** Sandra **(b)** Markus
 (c) Sandra **(d)** Markus

Grammar

Gender and plurals

A
1. der Mülleimer
2. das Kino
3. die Krankenschwester
4. der Rucksack
5. das Handy
6. das Restaurant
7. die Autobahn
8. der Sportlehrer
9. die Umwelt

B
1. Das Haus ist modern.
2. Der Schüler heißt Max.
3. Die Schülerin heißt Demet.
4. Der Computer ist kaputt.
5. Der Zug fährt langsam.
6. Die Sparkasse ist geschlossen.
7. Die Zeitung kostet 1 Euro.
8. Das Buch ist langweilig.

C
1. Wir haben die Pizza gegessen.
2. Wir können das Krankenhaus sehen.
3. Ich mache die Hausaufgabe.
4. Vati kauft den Pullover.
5. Liest du das Buch?
6. Ich mähe den Rasen.

D Haus S, Buch S, Männer P, Autos P, Häuser P, Supermarkt S, Tisch S, Mann S, Supermärkte P, Tische P, Handys P, Zimmer E, Bilder P, Computer E

Cases 1

A
1. um die Ecke
2. durch die Stadt
3. ohne ein Auto
4. für die Schule
5. für einen Freund
6. gegen die Wand
7. durch einen Wald

B
1. mit dem Bus
2. seit dem Sommer
3. zu der Bank / zur Bank
4. nach der Party
5. bei einem Freund / beim Freund
6. von einem Onkel / vom Onkel
7. gegenüber der Tankstelle
8. außer der Lehrerin

C
1. wegen des Wetters
2. während der Stunde
3. trotz des Regens

Cases 2

A
1. Wir fahren in die Stadt.
2. Meine Schwester ist in der Schule.
3. Das Essen liegt auf dem Tisch.
4. Ich steige auf die Mauer.
5. Wir hängen das Bild an die Wand.
6. Jetzt ist das Bild an der Wand.
7. Die Katze läuft hinter einen Schrank.
8. Wo ist die Katze jetzt? Hinter dem Schrank.
9. Die Bäckerei steht zwischen einem Supermarkt und einer Post.
10. Das Flugzeug fliegt über die Stadt. **OR** Das Flugzeug fliegt über der Stadt.
11. Ich stelle die Flaschen in den Schrank.
12. Der Bus steht an der Haltestelle.

B
1. Die Kinder streiten sich über das Fernsehprogramm.
2. Wir freuen uns auf das Festival.
3. Ich ärgere mich oft über die Arbeit.
4. Martin hat sich an die Sonne gewöhnt.
5. Wie lange warten Sie auf die Straßenbahn?

1. The children are arguing about the TV programme.
2. We are looking forward to the festival.
3. I often get cross about work.
4. Martin has got used to the sun.
5. How long have you been waiting for the tram?

C
1. auf dem Land – in the country
2. vor allem – above all
3. auf die Nerven – on my nerves
4. auf der rechten Seite – on the right
5. im Internet – on the internet

Cases 3

A
1. *this man* – dieser Mann
2. *with this man* – mit diesem Mann
3. *this woman* – diese Frau
4. *for this woman* – für diese Frau
5. *that horse* – jenes Pferd
6. *on that horse* – auf jenem Pferd

B 1 Unsere Schwester heißt Monika.
2 Ich habe keinen Bruder.
3 Meine Schule ist nicht sehr groß.
4 Hast du deinen Laptop vergessen?
5 Wie ist ihr Name, bitte? *(No ending necessary)*
6 Meine Lehrerin hat ihre Schulbücher nicht mit.
7 Wo steht Ihr Auto? *(No ending necessary)*
8 Wir arbeiten in unserem Büro.
9 Wo ist eure Wohnung? *(Note spelling change)*
10 Meine Lieblingsfächer sind Mathe und Informatik.
11 Wie heißt deine Freundin?
12 Leider haben wir keine Zeit.
13 Ihre E-Mail war nicht sehr höflich.
14 Olaf geht mit seinem Freund spazieren.
15 Madonna singt ihre besten Hits.
16 Wo habt ihr euer Auto stehen lassen? *(No ending necessary)*
17 Ich habe keine Ahnung.
18 Ich habe keine Lust.
19 Das war mein Fehler.
20 Meiner Meinung nach …

Adjective endings
A 1 Die intelligente Schülerin bekommt gute Noten.
2 Wir fahren mit dem nächsten Bus in die Stadt.
3 Hast du den gelben Vogel gesehen?
4 Der altmodische Lehrer ist streng.
5 Ich kaufe dieses schwarze Kleid.
6 Die neugebauten Reihenhäuser sind schön.
7 Heute gehen wir in den modernen Freizeitpark.
8 Wir müssen dieses schmutzige Fahrrad sauber machen.
9 Morgen gehen wir ins neue Einkaufszentrum.
10 Der verspätete Zug kommt um ein Uhr an.

B 1 München ist eine umweltfreundliche Stadt.
2 Ich suche ein preiswertes T-Shirt.
3 Marta hat ihre modische Handtasche verloren.
4 Wir haben unsere schwierigen Hausaufgaben nicht gemacht.
5 Ich habe ein bequemes Bett gekauft.
6 Das ist ein großes Problem.
7 Das war vielleicht eine langweilige Stunde!
8 Diese idiotischen Leute haben das Spiel verdorben.
9 Mein Vater hat einen schweren Unfall gehabt.
10 Klaus liebt seine neue Freundin.
11 Wir haben kein frisches Obst.
12 Maria hat einen grünen Mantel gekauft.

Comparisons
A 1 Mathe ist langweilig, Physik ist langweiliger, aber das langweiligste Fach ist Kunst.
2 Oliver läuft schnell, Ali läuft schneller, aber Tim läuft am schnellsten.
3 Berlin ist schön, Paris ist schöner, aber Venedig ist die schönste Stadt.
4 Madonna ist cool, Lady Gaga ist cooler, aber Beyoncé ist die coolste Sängerin.
5 Metallica ist lauter als Guns 'n' Roses.
6 Bremen ist kleiner als Hamburg.
7 Deine Noten sind schlecht, aber meine sind noch schlechter.
8 Ich finde Englisch einfacher als Französisch, aber Deutsch finde ich am einfachsten.
9 Skifahren ist schwieriger als Radfahren.
10 Mein Auto ist billiger als dein Auto, aber das Auto meines Vaters ist am billigsten.

B 1 Ich bin jünger als du.
2 Die Alpen sind höher als der Snowdon.
3 München ist größer als Bonn.
4 Meine Haare sind lang, Timos Haare sind länger, aber deine Haare sind am längsten.
5 Fußball ist gut, Handball ist besser, aber Tennis ist das beste Spiel.

1 I am younger than you.
2 The Alps are higher than Snowdon.
3 Munich is bigger than Bonn.
4 My hair is long, Timo's hair is longer but your hair is the longest.
5 Football is good, handball is better but tennis is the best game.

C 1 Ich spiele gern Korbball.
2 Ich esse lieber Gemüse als Fleisch.
3 Am liebsten gehe ich schwimmen.

Personal pronouns

A 1 Ich liebe dich.
2 Liebst du mich?
3 Kommst du mit mir?
4 Mein Bruder ist nett. Ich mag ihn gern.
5 Ich habe keine Kreditkarte. Ich habe sie verloren.
6 Ein Geschenk für uns? Danke!
7 Wir haben euch gestern gesehen.
8 Haben Sie gut geschlafen?
9 Die Party ist bei mir.
10 Rolf hat Hunger. Ich bin mit ihm essen gegangen.
11 Vergiss mich nicht!
12 Wie heißt du?
13 Wie heißen Sie?
14 Meine Schwester ist krank. Gestern sind wir zu ihr gegangen.
15 Was ist los mit dir?

B 1 Schwimmen fällt mir schwer.
2 Mmmm, Eis! Schmeckt es dir?
3 Aua! Das tut mir weh!
4 Leider geht es uns nicht gut.
5 Wer gewinnt im Fußball? Das ist mir egal.
6 Es tut uns leid.

Word order

A 1 Um sechs Uhr beginnt die Fernsehsendung.
2 Jeden Tag fahre ich mit dem Bus zur Arbeit.
3 Leider sind meine Eltern krank.
4 Hier darf man nicht rauchen.

B 1 Gestern haben wir Eis gegessen.
2 Manchmal ist Timo ins Kino gegangen.
3 Letztes Jahr ist Ali nach Frankreich gefahren.
4 Heute Morgen hast du Pommes gekauft.

C 1 Ich fahre jeden Tag mit dem Rad zur Schule.
2 Gehst du am Wochenende mit mir zum Schwimmbad?
3 Wir sehen oft im Wohnzimmer fern.
4 Mehmet spielt abends im Jugendklub Tischtennis.
5 Mein Vater arbeitet seit 20 Jahren fleißig im Büro.
6 Willst du heute Abend mit mir im Restaurant Pizza essen?

Conjunctions

A 1 Claudia will Sportlehrerin werden, weil sie sportlich ist.
2 Ich kann dich nicht anrufen, weil ich mein Handy verloren habe.
3 Wir fahren nach Spanien, weil das Wetter dort so schön ist.
4 Du darfst nicht im Garten spielen, weil es regnet.
5 Peter hat seine Hausaufgaben nicht gemacht, weil er faul ist.
6 Ich mag Computerspiele, weil sie so aufregend sind.

B 1 Du kannst abwaschen, während ich koche.
2 Wir kaufen oft ein, wenn wir in der Stadt sind.
3 Ich kann nicht zur Party kommen, da ich arbeiten werde.
4 Lasst uns früh aufstehen, damit wir wandern können.
5 Meine Eltern waren böse, obwohl ich nicht spät nach Hause gekommen bin.
6 Ich habe es nicht gewusst, dass du krank bist.
7 Papa hat geraucht, als er jung war.
8 Ich weiß nicht, wie man einen Computer repariert.
9 Wir können schwimmen gehen, wenn das Wetter gut ist.
10 Wir müssen warten, bis es nicht mehr regnet.

More on word order

A 1 Wir fahren in die Stadt, um Lebensmittel zu kaufen.
2 Viele Leute spielen Tennis, um fit zu werden.
3 Boris spart Geld, um ein Motorrad zu kaufen.
4 Meine Schwester geht zur Abendschule, um Französisch zu lernen.
5 Ich bin gestern zum Imbiss gegangen, um Pommes zu essen.

B 1 Das Orchester beginnt zu spielen.
2 Wir hoffen, Spanisch zu lernen.
3 Oliver versucht, Gitarre zu spielen.

C 1 das Mädchen, das Tennis spielt
2 der Junge, der gut singt
3 der Mann, der Deutsch spricht
4 das Haus, das alt ist
5 das Fach, das schwer ist
6 das Auto, das kaputt ist
7 die Tasse, die voll ist

The present tense

A 1 wir gehen 2 er findet
3 sie singt 4 ich spiele
5 ihr macht 6 du sagst
7 es kommt 8 sie schwimmen
9 ich höre 10 wir trinken

B 1 Was liest du?
2 Schläfst du?
3 Annabelle isst nicht gern Fleisch.
4 Kerstin spricht gut Englisch.
5 Nimmst du Zucker?
6 Ben fährt bald nach Berlin.
7 Hilfst du mir, bitte?
8 Mein Onkel gibt mir 20 Euro.

1 What are you reading?
2 Are you asleep?
3 Annabelle doesn't like eating meat.
4 Kerstin speaks English well.
5 Do you take sugar?
6 Ben is going to Berlin soon.
7 Will you help me please?
8 My uncle is giving me 20 euros.

C er spricht, du siehst, sie fährt, er liest

More on verbs

A 1 Wir waschen ab.
2 Er wacht um 7 Uhr auf.
3 Wir laden oft Filme herunter.
4 Wie oft siehst du fern?
5 Wo steigt man aus?
6 Ich wasche nie ab.

B 1 Wir haben abgewaschen.
2 Er ist um 7 Uhr aufgewacht.
3 Wir haben oft Filme heruntergeladen.
4 Wie oft hast du ferngesehen?
5 Wo ist man ausgestiegen?
6 Ich habe nie abgewaschen.

C 1 Ich interessiere mich für Geschichte.
2 Sara freut sich auf die Ferien.
3 Erinnerst du dich an mich?
4 Wir langweilen uns in der Schule.
5 Ich habe mich noch nicht entschieden.
6 Dieter hat sich heute noch nicht rasiert.
7 Habt ihr euch gut amüsiert?
8 Unser Haus befindet sich in der Nähe vom Bahnhof.

1 I am interested in history.
2 Sara is looking forward to the holidays.
3 Do you remember me?
4 We get bored at school.
5 I haven't decided yet.
6 Dieter hasn't shaved yet today.
7 Have you enjoyed yourselves?
8 Our house is situated near the train station.

Commands

A 1 Parken Sie hier nicht!
2 Sprechen Sie nicht so laut!
3 Steigen Sie hier aus!
4 Fahren Sie nicht so schnell!
5 Kommen Sie herein!
6 Gehen Sie geradeaus!
7 Kommen Sie bald wieder!
8 Geben Sie mir 10 Euro!

B 1 Steh auf!
2 Schreib bald!
3 Komm her!
4 Nimm zwei!
5 Bring mir den Ball!
6 Hör auf!
7 Benimm dich!
8 Setz dich!

Present tense modals

A 1 Ich kann nicht schnell laufen.
2 Wir müssen bald Kaffee kaufen.
3 Kinder sollten keinen Alkohol trinken.
4 Claudia mag nicht schwimmen.
5 Schüler dürfen hier nicht sitzen.
6 Wir wollen Pommes essen.
7 Hier darf man parken.
8 Meine Eltern wollen eine neue Wohnung kaufen.
9 Du kannst gut Fußball spielen.
10 Sie sollten höflich sein.

B 1 Im Kino darf man nicht rauchen.
2 Wir möchten zur Bowlingbahn gehen.
3 Meine Freunde wollen zu Hause bleiben.
4 Ihr müsst weniger essen.
5 Man soll nicht viel Zucker essen.
6 Ergül kann gut Gitarre spielen.
7 Kannst du mir mit meinen Hausaufgaben helfen?
8 Man darf den Rasen nicht betreten.
9 Wir müssen mit der Straßenbahn fahren.
10 Ich will meinen Salat nicht essen.

Imperfect modals

A 1 ich wollte   2 wir mussten
3 sie konnten   4 sie durfte
5 man sollte   6 er mochte
7 wir wollten   8 Jutta konnte

B 1 Du solltest gesund essen.
2 Wir mussten nach Hause gehen.
3 Ella mochte nicht Musik hören.
4 Wir wollten im Internet surfen.
5 Ich konnte gut Tischtennis spielen.
6 Ihr durftet spät ins Bett gehen.

C 1 Möchten Sie Tennis spielen?
2 Wir könnten einkaufen gehen.
3 Ich möchte ein Eis essen.
4 Könntest du mir helfen?

The perfect tense 1

A 1 Wir haben Minigolf gespielt.
2 Habt ihr neue Schuhe gekauft?
3 Hast du deine Oma besucht?
4 Was hat er gesagt?
5 Ich habe Spanisch gelernt.
6 Hast du Harry Potter gelesen?
7 Dennis hat mir ein Geschenk gegeben.
8 Wir haben einen tollen Film gesehen.

B 1 Wohin bist du gefahren?
2 Wir sind nach Mallorca gefahren.
3 Ich bin zu Hause geblieben.
4 Usain Bolt ist schnell gelaufen.
5 Meine Mutter ist nach Amerika geflogen.
6 Der Zug ist abgefahren.

C 1 Abdul hat 12 Stunden geschlafen.
2 Wir haben unsere Hausaufgaben gemacht.
3 Wohin bist du gefahren?
4 Ich bin spät nach Hause gekommen.
5 Habt ihr Britta gesehen?

The perfect tense 2

A 1 geschwommen   2 gewesen
3 geschlossen   4 gegessen
5 gestanden   6 gesessen
7 geschrieben   8 gestorben
9 gesprochen   10 getroffen
11 geworden   12 getrunken
13 genommen   14 gesungen
15 gehabt

B 1 Wir haben eine E-Mail geschrieben.
2 Wir haben uns um 6 Uhr getroffen.
3 Mein Onkel ist gestorben.
4 Hast du mein Handy genommen?
5 Ich habe eine Bratwurst gegessen.
6 Er hat ein Glas Cola getrunken.
7 Wir sind im Meer geschwommen.
8 Marita hat Italienisch gesprochen.

C 1 vergessen   2 aufgestanden
3 empfohlen   4 verloren
5 besucht   6 heruntergeladen
7 abgefahren   8 ausgestiegen

The imperfect tense

A 1 Ich spielte am Computer.
2 Was sagtest du?
3 Nina kaufte Kaugummi.
4 Die Schüler lernten Englisch.
5 Es schneite im Winter.
6 Peter lachte laut.

B 1 Es war gestern kalt.
2 Wir hatten auf der Party viel Spaß.
3 Paul war im Krankenhaus.
4 Meine Eltern hatten drei Kinder.
5 Ich war gestern im Imbiss.
6 Hattest du Angst?

C 1 Es gab viel zu essen. I
2 Wir sitzen im Kino. P
3 Es tut mir leid! P
4 Ich fahre nach Berlin. P
5 Er kommt früh an. P
6 Er saß im Wohnzimmer. I
7 Sie kamen um 6 Uhr an. I
8 Wie findest du das? P
9 Aua! Das tat weh! I
10 Ich fand es gut. I
11 Es gibt nicht viel zu tun. P
12 Klaus fuhr zu schnell. I

The future tense

A 1 Susi geht nächstes Jahr auf die Uni.
    2 Wir fahren im Sommer nach Ibiza.
    3 Er kommt übermorgen zu uns.
    4 Ich bleibe heute Abend zu Hause.
    5 Bringst du am Wochenende deine Schwester mit?

B 1 Ich werde um 6 Uhr aufstehen.
    2 Wirst du am Wochenende Musik hören?
    3 Werdet ihr Pizza essen?
    4 Wir werden die Prüfung bestehen.
    5 Nächstes Jahr werden wir nach Afrika fahren.
    6 Daniel wird einen Film herunterladen.
    7 Ich werde ein Problem mit meinem Laptop haben.
    8 Bayern München wird das Spiel gewinnen.
    9 Meine Freunde werden um 9 Uhr ankommen.
    10 Meine Schwester wird im August heiraten.

C *Answers variable!*

The conditional

A 1 Wenn wir Zeit hätten, würden wir einkaufen gehen.
    2 Wenn meine Eltern Geld hätten, würden sie ein Auto kaufen.
    3 Wenn ich Kinder hätte, würde ich sie lieben.
    4 Wenn Tanja nicht krank wäre, würde sie Skateboard fahren.
    5 Wenn du fleißiger wärst, würdest du deine Prüfung bestehen.
    6 Wenn das Wetter besser wäre, würden wir Sport treiben.

B 1 Wenn ich Krankenschwester wäre, würde ich mich freuen.
    2 Wenn er Klempner wäre, würde er viel verdienen.
    3 Wenn wir in einer Fabrik arbeiten würden, wären wir müde.
    4 Wenn wir Glasflaschen hätten, würden wir sie recyceln.
    5 Wenn ich Hunger hätte, würde ich eine Bratwurst essen.
    6 Wenn Manya und Timo Talent hätten, würden sie in einer Band spielen.

C *Answers variable!*

D *Answers variable!*

The pluperfect tense

A 1 Wir hatten Kaffee und Kuchen bestellt.
    2 Hattest du Spaß gehabt?
    3 Ich hatte eine neue Stelle bekommen.
    4 Wir hatten unsere Freunde eingeladen.
    5 Als ich nach Hause gekommen war, habe ich gegessen.
    6 Ergül war zur Bäckerei gegangen.
    7 Sie waren zu Hause geblieben.
    8 Ich war mit dem Auto nach Frankfurt gefahren.

B 1 Es war nicht passiert.
    2 Ich hatte dir eine E-Mail geschickt.
    3 Hattest du dich nicht rasiert?
    4 Ich war sehr früh eingeschlafen.
    5 Opa war noch nie nach London gefahren.
    6 Warst du zur Haltestelle gegangen?
    7 Wir hatten unseren Müll zur Mülldeponie gebracht.
    8 Er hatte zwei Computerspiele heruntergeladen.
    9 Die Fabrik war geschlossen worden.
    10 Fatima hatte Abitur gemacht.

Questions

A 1 Spielt Kevin oft am Computer?
    2 Hast du dein Handy verloren?
    3 Wollen wir Volleyball spielen?
    4 Studiert Hakan Informatik?
    5 Geht ihr morgen zum Sportzentrum?

B 1 Bist du zum Supermarkt gefahren?
    2 Wird Ayse Chemie studieren?
    3 Ist dein Auto kaputt?
    4 Isst du gern Bratwurst mit Pommes?
    5 Wird es morgen regnen?

C *who?* – wer?   *what?* – was?   *how?* – wie?   *when?* – wann?   *why?* – warum?   *where?* – wo?
how many? – wie viele?
what kind of? – was für?
whose? – wessen?
who with? – mit wem?

D *Answers variable!*

Time markers

A
1 gestern – *past*
2 früher – *past*
3 bald – *future*
4 letzte Woche – *past*
5 heute – *present*
6 normalerweise – *present*
7 vor 2 Wochen – *past*
8 morgen – *future*
9 nächste Woche – *future*
10 jetzt – *present*

B
manchmal – *sometimes*
neulich – *recently*
sofort – *immediately*
täglich – *every day*
rechtzeitig – *on time*
in Zukunft – *in the future*

C
1 Nächste Woche werde ich mein Betriebspraktikum machen.
2 Heute Abend sieht Ulli fern.
3 In Zukunft wird man Strom sparen.
4 Bald wirst du einen Unfall haben.
5 Manchmal treffen wir uns mit unseren Freunden.
6 Neulich war ich bei meinem Onkel.
7 Vorgestern hat Mehmet sein Betriebspraktikum begonnen.
8 Jeden Tag gehe ich zur Bäckerei.

Numbers

A
1 421
2 1644
3 68
4 301
5 97
6 105
7 17
8 653

B
1 Es ist zwanzig nach neun. (20, 9)
2 Ausverkauf! Fünfzehn Prozent Rabatt! (15)
3 Es ist dreizehn Grad. (13)
4 Ich habe sechshundertfünfzig Euro gewonnen. (650)
5 Der Zug kommt um zwölf Minuten vor sieben an. (12, 7)
6 Es gibt dreißig Schüler in meiner Klasse. (30)

C
1 12.3.   2 13.7.   3 28.12.
4 1.4.   5 3.1.   6 17.6.

D
1 Mein Geburtstag ist am ersten November.
2 Saschas Geburtstag ist am siebten September.
3 Das Konzert findet am zwölften Mai statt.
4 Die Ferien beginnen am zweiten Juli.

Practice Exam Paper

Reading

1 **(i)** D   **(ii)** B   **(iii)** F   **(iv)** C
2 **(i)** D   **(ii)** F   **(iii)** G   **(iv)** B
3 **(i)** C   **(ii)** F   **(iii)** D   **(iv)** E
4 **(a)** 5   **(b)** noisy/loud
  (c) funny   **(d)** curly
5 **(i)** C   **(ii)** A   **(iii)** B   **(iv)** E
6 **(a)** Past   **(b)** Future
  (c) Present   **(d)** Past
7 **(a)** Esma   **(b)** Ben
  (b) Mehmet   **(d)** Hanna
8 **(a)** for the German students to improve their English
  (b) to save money
  (c) write an essay about English schools
  (d) can stay in bed longer/get up later
  (e) students don't have to repeat a year
  (f) they don't want them
  (g) he bought a school jumper
  (h) giving a talk (in German class) / talking about German schools (in class)
9 **A (a)** (ii)   **(b)** (iii)
    (c) (ii)   **(d)** (i)
  B (b) (e) (f) (h)

Listening

1 **(1)** (iii)   **(2)** (iii)   **(3)** (i)   **(4)** (ii)
2 **(1)** (ii)   **(2)** (ii)   **(3)** (iii)   **(4)** (i)
3 B E F G
4 **(i)** C, A   **(ii)** I   **(iii)** D
5 Martha – (iii)   Benjamin – (i)
  Danni – (iv)   Kevin – (ii)
6 **(a)** (ii)   **(b)** (ii)   **(c)** (iii)   **(d)** (i)
7 **(i)** D   **(ii)** F   **(iii)** A   **(iv)** E
8 (b) (d) (f) (h)
9 **(a)** holiday destination for ski fans
  (b) (i) 128 km of ski slopes or 57 ski slopes
    (ii) fantastic views
  (c) people who want to learn a water sport (surfing, diving, sailing)
10 (b) (d) (e) (h)

Your own notes

Published by Pearson Education Limited, 80 Strand, London, WC2R 0RL.

www.pearsonschoolsandfecolleges.co.uk

Copies of official specifications for all Edexcel qualifications may be found on the Edexcel website: www.edexcel.com

Text © Pearson Education Limited 2013
Audio © Pearson Education Limited / Tom Dick and Debbie Productions
MFL Series Editor: Julie Green
Edited by Jenny Draine and Sue Chapple
Typeset by Kamae Design, Oxford
Original illustrations © Pearson Education Limited 2013
Illustrated by KJA Artists
Cover illustration by Miriam Sturdee

The rights of Olwyn Bowpitt, Oliver Gray, Alan O'Brien and Harriette Lanzer to be identified as authors of this work have been asserted by them in accordance with the Copyright, Designs and Patents Act 1988.

First published 2013

16
10 9 8 7 6 5

British Library Cataloguing in Publication Data
A catalogue record for this book is available from the British Library

ISBN 978 1 446 90348 3

Printed in Slovakia by Neografia

In the writing of this book, no Edexcel examiners authored sections relevant to examination papers for which they have responsibility.